REVIEWS OF UNITED KINGDOM
STATISTICAL SOURCES

Volume XIII

WAGES AND EARNINGS

REVIEWS OF UNITED KINGDOM STATISTICAL SOURCES

Editor: W. F. Maunder

REVIEWS OF UNITED KINGDOM STATISTICAL SOURCES

Edited by W. F. MAUNDER

Professor of Economic and Social Statistics
University of Exeter

VOLUME XIII

WAGES AND EARNINGS

by

ANDREW DEAN

Organisation for Economic Cooperation and Development
formerly at the
National Institute of Economic and Social Research

Published for
The Royal Statistical Society and
the Social Science Research Council

by

PERGAMON PRESS

OXFORD · NEW YORK · TORONTO · SYDNEY · PARIS · FRANKFURT

U.K.	Pergamon Press Ltd., Headington Hill Hall, Oxford OX3 0BW, England
U.S.A.	Pergamon Press Inc., Maxwell House, Fairview Park, Elmsford, New York 10523, U.S.A.
CANADA	Pergamon of Canada, Suite 104, 150 Consumers Road, Willowdale, Ontario M2J 1P9, Canada
AUSTRALIA	Pergamon Press (Aust.) Pty. Ltd., P.O. Box 544, Potts Point, N.S.W. 2011, Australia
FRANCE	Pergamon Press SARL, 24 rue des Ecoles, 75240 Paris, Cedex 05, France
FEDERAL REPUBLIC OF GERMANY	Pergamon Press GmbH, 6242 Kronberg/Taunus, Pferdstrasse 1, Federal Republic of Germany

First Edition 1980

British Library Cataloguing in Publication Data

Reviews of United Kingdom statistical sources.
Vol. 13: Wages and earnings
1. Great Britain—Statistical services.
I. Maunder, Wayne Frederick   II. Dean, Andrew
III. Royal Statistical Society
IV. Social Science Research Council, Great Britain
314.1   HA37.G7   79-40929

ISBN 0-08-024060-7

For Bibliographic purposes this volume should be cited as:
Dean, Andrew, *Wages and Earnings,* Pergamon Press Limited
on behalf of the Royal Statistical Society and the Social Science
Research Council, 1980

Printed and bound in Great Britain by
William Clowes (Beccles) Limited, Beccles and London

VOLUME CONTENTS

FOREWORD

The Sources and Nature of the Statistics of the United Kingdom, produced under the auspices of the Royal Statistical Society and edited by Maurice Kendall, filled a notable gap on the library shelves when it made its appearance in the early post-war years. Through a series of critical reviews by many of the foremost national experts, it constituted a valuable contemporary guide to statisticians working in many fields as well as a bench-mark to which historians of the development of Statistics in this country are likely to return again and again. The Social Science Research Council and the Society were both delighted when Professor Maunder came forward with the proposal that a revised version should be produced, indicating as well his willingness to take on the onerous task of editor. The two bodies were more than happy to act as co-sponsors of the project and to help in its planning through a joint steering committee. The result, we are confident, will be adjudged a worthy successor to the previous volumes by the very much larger 'statistics public' that has come into being in the intervening years.

Dr C. S. Smith

Secretary
Social Science Research Council

April 1979

Dr I. D. Hill

Honorary Secretary
Royal Statistical Society

April 1979

MEMBERSHIP OF THE JOINT STEERING COMMITTEE
(April 1979)

Chairman: Miss S. V. Cunliffe

Representing the Royal Statistical Society:
Mr M. C. Fessey
Prof. H. Goldstein
Dr S. Rosenbaum

Representing the Social Research Council:
Mr A. S. Noble
Mrs J. Peretz
Dr W. Taylor

Secretary: Mr D. E. Allen

INTRODUCTION

The question of priorities and of balance as between economic and social topics in the series as a whole has been the subject of previous introductory comment and is a question of policy which is kept under constant scrutiny. In presenting this volume it may be claimed without much hesitation that it is a happy non-problem in that the subject must surely be a prime candidate for inclusion from both the economic and social aspects. Moreover, the treatment of Wages and Earnings is a natural sequel to the more general coverage of Wealth and Incomes in Volume VI and this is a point which the present contributor explains in detail.

Writing with regard to the series generally, the primary aim is to act as a work of reference to the sources of statistical material of all kinds, both official and unofficial. It seeks to enable the user to discover what data are available on the subject in which he is interested, from where they may be obtained, and what the limitations are to their use. Data are regarded as available not only if published in the normal printed format but also if they are likely to be released to a *bona fide* enquirer in any other form, such as duplicated documents, computer print-out, or even magnetic tape. On the other hand, no reference is made to material which, even if it is known to exist, is not accessible to the general run of potential users. The distinction, of course, is not clear-cut and mention of a source is not to be regarded as a guarantee that data will be released; in particular cases it may very well be a matter for negotiation. The latter caution applies with particular force to the question of obtaining computer print-outs of custom specified tabulations. Where original records are held on magnetic tape it might appear that there should be no insuperable problem, apart from confidentiality, in obtaining any feasible analysis at a cost; in practice, it may well turn out that there are capacity restraints which override any simple cost calculation. Thus, what is requested might make demands on computer and programming resources to the extent that the routine work of the agency concerned would be intolerably affected.

The intention is that the sources for each topic should be reviewed in detail, and the brief supplied to authors has called for comprehensive coverage at the level of 'national interest'. This term does not denote any necessary restriction to statistics collected on a national basis (still less, of course, to national aggregates) but it means that sources of a purely local character, without wider interest in either content or methodology, are excluded. Indeed, the mere task of identifying all material of this latter kind is an impossibility. The interpretation of the brief has obviously involved discretion and it is up to the users of these reviews to say what unreasonable gaps become apparent to them. They are cordially invited to do so by communicating with me.

To facilitate the use of the series as a work of reference, certain features have been incorporated which are worth a word or two of explanation.

First, the text of each review is designed, in so far as varying subject-matter permits, to follow a standard form of arrangement so that users may expect a similar pattern to be followed throughout the series. The starting-point is a brief summary of the activity concerned and its organization, in order to give a clear background understanding of how data are collected, what is being measured, the stage at which measurements are made, what the reporting units are, the channels through which returns are routed, and where they are processed. As a further part of this introductory material, there is a discussion of the specific problems of definition and measurement to which the topic gives rise. The core sections on available sources which follow are arranged at the author's discretion—by origin, by subject subdivision, or by type of data; there is too much heterogeneity between topics to permit any imposition of complete uniformity on all authors. The final section is devoted to a discussion of general shortcomings and possibly desirable improvements. In case a contrary expectation should be aroused, it should be said that authors have not been asked to produce a comprehensive plan for the reform of statistical reporting in the whole of their field. However, a review of existing sources is a natural opportunity to make some suggestions for future policy on the collection and publication of statistics within the scope concerned.

Secondly, detailed factual information about statistical series and other data is given in a Quick Reference List (QRL). The exact nature of the entries is best seen by glancing at the list and accordingly they are not described here. Again, the ordering is not prescribed except that entries are not classified by publication source since it is presumed that it is this which is unknown to the reader. In general, the routine type of information which is given in the QRL is not repeated verbally in the text; the former, however, serves as a search route to the latter in that a reference (by section number) is shown against a QRL entry when there is a related discussion in the text.

Thirdly, a subject index to each review acts as a more or less conventional line of enquiry on textual references; however, it is a computerized system and, for an individual review, the only peculiarity which it introduces is the possibility of easily permuting entries. Thus an entry in the index may appear as:

National wage settlements

and also be shown as:

Wage settlements, national

as well as:

Settlements, national wage

The object at this level is merely to facilitate search by giving as many variants as possible. In addition, individual review subject indexes are merged into a cumulative index which is held on magnetic tape and may possibly be used to produce a printed version from time to time if that seems desirable. Computer print-outs of the cumulative index to date are available on application to me at the Department of Economics, University of Exeter. In addition, selective searches of this index may be made by the input of key-words; the result is a print-out of all entries in which the key-word appears in the initial position in the subject index of any review. Like the cumulative index itself, this is a facility which may be of increasing help as the number of reviews in print grows.

Fourthly, each review contains two listings of publications. The QRL Key gives full details of the publications shown as sources and text references to them are made in the form [QRL serial number]; this list is confined essentially to data publications. The other listing is a general bibliography of works discussing wider aspects; text references in this case are made in the form [B serial number].

Finally, an attempt is made to reproduce the more important returns or forms used in data collection so that it may be seen what tabulations it is possible to make as well as helping to clarify the basis of those actually available. Unfortunately, there are severe practical limitations on the number of such forms that it is possible to append to a review and authors perforce have to be highly selective.

If all or any of these features succeed in their intention of increasing the value of the series in its basic function as a work of reference it will be gratifying; the extent to which the purpose is achieved, however, will be difficult to assess without 'feedback' from the readership. Users, therefore, will be rendering an essential service if they will send me a note of specific instances where, in consulting a review, they have failed to find the information sought.

As editor, I must express my very grateful thanks to all the members of the Joint Steering Committee of the Royal Statistical Society and the Social Science Research Council. It would be unfair to saddle them with any responsibility for shortcomings in execution but they have directed the overall strategy with as admirable a mixture of guidance and forbearance as any editor of such a series could desire. Especial thanks are due to the Secretary of the Committee who is an unfailing source of help even when sorely pressed by the more urgent demands of his other offices.

The author joins me in thanking all those who gave up their time to attend the seminar held to discuss the first drafts of this review and who contributed materially to improving the final version. We are most grateful to Mr Thomas Dalby of Pergamon Press Ltd. for all his help, particularly during the vital production stages. The subject index entries for this volume were compiled by Mrs Juliet Horwood who has also been responsible for many other aspects of the work. Our thanks go also to Mrs Gill Skinner, of the Social Studies Data Processing Unit at the University of Exeter, who has written the computer programs for the production of the subject indexes. Finally, we also wish to record our appreciation for permission granted to produce certain Copyright material by the Controller of Her Majesty's Stationery Office.

W. F. MAUNDER

University of Exeter
April 1979

23: WAGES AND EARNINGS

ANDREW DEAN

*Organisation for Economic Cooperation and Development, formerly
at the National Institute of Economic and
Social Research*

REFERENCE DATE OF SOURCES REVIEWED

This review is believed to represent the position, broadly speaking, as it obtained at December 1978. Later revisions have been inserted up to the proof-reading stage (November 1979), taking account, as far as possible, of major changes in the situation.

ADDENDUM

1. Index to *Gazette* statistics
   Since October 1979 the Department of Employment has published at the back of each *Gazette* a list of the statistics on wages, earnings and labour costs which appear regularly in the publication. The frequency with which each series is published, the table number (if relevant), and the date and page number of the latest issue in which the statistics appear are all listed. This is a most useful and welcome innovation which should make it much easier to find the most recent data.

2. Royal Commission on the Distribution of Income and Wealth (section 3.3.3)
   The Royal Commission was abolished by the Conservative Government in 1979.

3. *New Earnings Survey 1979*
   The April 1979 NES included additional questions to meet the requirements of the EEC for comparative information on the structure and distribution of earnings in industry and commerce in the Community countries (October 1979 *Gazette,* page 965). The EEC 'Structure of Earnings' surveys were carried out in 1966, 1972 and 1978, with large samples of employees, and the Department of Employment attempted to adapt the NES to provide the necessary information. The main part of the questionnaire remained as before, but additional questions were asked on the classification of the business in the NACE system, the number of employees, the employee's earnings in the previous 12 months and the job category of the employee. Detailed analysis of this data, in addition to the normal NES results, will be published by the Statistical Office of the European Communities in the Eurostat series; but since the publication lag is so long, some of the new data will be published in advance in the *Gazette*.

LIST OF ABBREVIATIONS

AUEW	Amalgamated Union of Engineering Workers
CBI	Confederation of British Industry
CSO	Central Statistical Office
DHSS	Department of Health and Social Security
DMS	Department of Manpower Services
E	England
E & W	England and Wales
EEC	European Economic Community
FES	Family Expenditure Survey
Gazette	*Department of Employment Gazette* (formerly *Employment and Productivity Gazette,* and *Ministry of Labour Gazette)*
GHS	General Household Survey
GB	Great Britain
HMSO	Her Majesty's Stationery Office
IDS	Incomes Data Services
ILO	International Labour Organization
IPM	Institute of Personnel Management
ISIC	International Standards of Industrial Classification
KOS	Key Occupations for Statistical purposes
MLH	Minimum List Heading (of the SIC)
NALGO	National and Local Government Officers Association
NCB	National Coal Board
NES	New Earnings Survey
NI	Northern Ireland
OECD	Organization for Economic Co-operation and Development
OES	October Earnings Survey
OPCS	Office of Population Censuses and Surveys
PAYE	Pay-As-You-Earn
PBR	Payment by results
PER	Professional and Executive Recruitment
SIC	Standard Industrial Classification
TGWU	Transport and General Workers Union
TUC	Trades Union Congress
UK	United Kingdom
UN	United Nations
W	Wales
WEU	Western European Union

ACKNOWLEDGEMENTS

I am grateful for the very valuable help that I have received in preparing this volume from colleagues at the National Institute of Economic and Social Research, officials at the Department of Employment, Messrs. R. F. Elliott and J. L. Fallick of Aberdeen University, the staff of Income Data Services, and the series editor, Professor W. F. Maunder. I am also grateful to all the participants at the seminar held in August 1977 to discuss an early draft of this volume. The arduous task of typing and retyping successive drafts of the volume has been carried out with great efficiency and good humour by Mrs F. Robinson, to whom my especial thanks are due.

Much of the material on the official statistics is taken from official descriptions published in the *Gazette* and elsewhere. The use of this material, the sources of which are cited in the text, is gratefully acknowledged.

The views expressed in this volume remain the sole responsibility of the author and should not be attributed to either the OECD or the National Institute.

CONTENTS OF REVIEW 23

CHAPTER 1

INTRODUCTION

1.1. Definitions

This review of statistical sources is concerned with the broad area of earnings from employment. It is *not* concerned with the self-employed or with total personal incomes, which are the subject of a separate review, see Stark [B 34]. The difference between these various concepts is a fine one, but we shall here try to explain the distinction.

In general, when we talk of personal incomes we are referring to payments received by individuals from all sources. Two major sources of such payments are incomes from employment and incomes from self-employment. The two of these are sometimes called 'earned incomes'. This is to distinguish these incomes, which accrue to the individual from some input of effort, from what are called 'unearned incomes', that is receipts such as rent, interest, dividends and grants. The topic of this volume is one component of personal incomes, albeit the largest one—namely, income from employment, which we shall henceforth refer to as earnings. The broader topic of personal incomes is covered by Stark [B 34]. His review is concerned largely with personal incomes as defined in a national income accounting framework (as in the table on total personal incomes in the annual Blue Book on *National Income and Expenditure* [QRL 53], for instance). The present review is concerned with only one of the twelve sub-divisions of total personal incomes in the national accounts; namely, wages and salaries. Wages and salaries plus the pay of the Armed Forces make up what is conventionally called 'income from employment'. Those who wish to find out about the statistical sources of other forms of personal incomes such as income from self-employment, property income, imputed income, or transfer incomes should refer to the review on *Personal Incomes* already mentioned [B 34]. That review is concerned with flows of money to persons and the way in which these are distributed, whilst a further review by Atkinson and Harrison on *Wealth* [B 1] deals with what we might consider as stocks of money or goods.

The concept of personal incomes is therefore a global one, and earnings are only one component. In this review we shall be dealing with just this one component and we shall be defining it in a fairly narrow sense. We shall in general be dealing with earnings from just one source, the individual's primary employment. If an individual holds two jobs then we regard him as having two sources of earnings and we shall be mainly concerned with the job which provides him with his major source of earned income. The first part of this review will be concerned with earnings in this narrow sense and with the concepts of wages and salaries. At the end of the review we shall go on to discuss employees' fringe benefits, with the associated concept of total remuneration, and employers' labour costs.

Whilst the distinction between incomes and earnings may seem rather difficult to grasp, that between the different concepts of earnings is even more difficult to describe. Traditionally wages have been regarded as the earnings of manual workers and shop assistants and salaries have been regarded as the earnings of all other non-manual workers. Thus earnings in the national accounting framework are described as 'wages and salaries'.

However, other definitions abound. Salaries are often described as monthly or annual payments. This definition becomes complicated when those who are regarded as 'wage-earners' are increasingly being paid on a monthly basis.

Yet another definition relates the wages/salaries distinction to performance. The wage rate represents a fixed level of remuneration for a fixed level of labour input, usually specified in terms of hours but sometimes in terms of work done (piece rates). On top of this basic wage rate for the standard hours of work done there may also be additional payment for extra hours, extra productivity, etc. The total of these payments is then known as the 'wages' of those workers, i.e. the total earnings for that employment. The basic wage rate, as we shall show later in Section 4.1, may therefore be only a part, albeit the major part, of wages as a whole. In contrast, the salary scale that an individual receives is practically the whole of the earnings of non-manual workers. Generally speaking, there is no reward for the 'salary-earner' for short-term variations in their labour input, since these are accepted as part of the initial contract. However, salaries are distinguished from wages in that they often involve increasing rewards to much more continuous increases in performance, which are perceptible only over longer time periods than in most manual employments and are consequently rewarded at longer intervals. These intervals are usually of one year, and the salary progression is set out in the form of an incremental scale. Salary increments are often paid almost as a matter of custom. Less frequently the incremental scale is known but increments are awarded on a discretionary basis.

The distinction between wages and salaries is one that has also been used in the past by the CSO in their breakdown of total personal incomes in the national income accounts. A classification of occupations between wage and salary earners by the General Register Office can be found in the *Sample Census 1966 (Great Britain) Economic Activity Tables* [B 42], Part III, page xlii. But since 1971 the split between wages and salaries has been dropped from the national income accounts because the distinction is difficult to draw and is somewhat arbitrary, although figures can still be obtained from the CSO for the period up to 1973.

So far we have mentioned various concepts—incomes, earnings, wages, and salaries—and we have pointed out that some of these expressions are used interchangeably. It is therefore important that the user of statistics should always be clear which concept he is using and that he should make this clear to others when he is reporting on any statistics. In this review when we mention *incomes* we shall be talking about the national income concept of personal incomes which is the subject of the Stark review [B 34]. The term *earnings* will be used to describe all cash payments received from the employer before deducting social security and tax contributions of the employees (this is the ILO definition). The term *wages* will be used to describe the earnings of manual workers and shop assistants, in contrast with *salaries*, which will describe the earnings of all other non-manual workers. Associated with each of these two types of earners, we will talk about *wage rates* and *salary scales*, which will refer to the basic rates or scales of payment by which the wage and salary earners are rewarded for their standard duties. On top of these wage rates or salary scales there are likely to be further payments in the form of overtime, bonus, commission, etc., which, taken together with basic pay (if any), will make up the total earnings of the individual concerned from the employment being considered. Such earnings therefore represent the total pay which employees receive from their employers *in the form of money* and before any deductions. They do not include income in kind, with the exception of coal-mining, agriculture, and catering, which will be mentioned further below. Nor do they include employers' contributions to national insurance and superannuation schemes (which *are* included in the CSO definition of personal incomes).

When, in addition, fringe benefits are added to earnings, we arrive at the concept of the employees' total remuneration. Finally, when employers' national insurance contributions and personnel costs are included, we arrive at labour costs—the total cost to the firm of employing labour. These concepts will also be examined later in the review.

1.2. Coverage of the Study

We have already indicated that most of the statistics which we shall consider are ones that have been compiled by government departments. The non-official sources which we shall consider relate mostly to salary statistics, but we shall also mention special studies where the official data have been reprocessed to give different series. Most of the official data are produced by the Department of Employment. The most important results are published in the *Department of Employment Gazette* [QRL 24], which has been published each month since May 1893 when it was first produced by the Labour Department of the Board of Trade and was known as the *Labour Gazette*. The major series published in the *Gazette* are also reproduced in *British Labour Statistics Year-books* [QRL 19], *Economic Trends* [QRL 27], the *Monthly Digest of Statistics* [QRL 52], and the *Annual Abstract of Statistics* [QRL 13], so there are several alternative sources for the official wage and earnings statistics.

This review will give most attention to the presently available statistics, but where possible we will mention sources for historical statistics as well. The main source for these statistics is *British Labour Statistics Historical Abstract, 1886–1968* [QRL 18], a volume which has brought together all of the more important historical statistical series in the labour field. We shall also refer to the *British Labour Statistics Yearbooks* [QRL 19], which are annual volumes published from 1969 onwards (i.e. following the *Historical Abstract*) which assemble all the important official statistical information on the labour market for the year in question. In general in each section we shall cover current statistical series fairly comprehensively and will then deal with the historical data in a separate chapter, usually giving only brief references to the sources for the latter material. The main emphasis will therefore be on post-war data, but references to earlier data will be given.

Since most of the official statistics have already been described in some detail in official publications we shall often give just brief descriptions of the data and their availability and refer the reader to the original official description for further details. On the occasions where we depart from this procedure the reason will be either that official information is not readily available or that the series is sufficiently important (e.g. the wage rates index) to merit a more detailed description.

As regards geographical coverage, we shall be discussing some fairly heterogeneous material. Some series will be for the whole of the United Kindgom whilst others will cover only some part of that area. In the case of each series we will specify the geographical area being considered. Additionally, we shall be pointing out the availability of regional data for some of the statistical series. We shall also mention some of the international data-collecting or data-collating agencies such as the EEC, the OECD, the ILO, and the UN. Usually these agencies just take their data from the member governments, but we shall see that in some special cases the official data are reprocessed to provide a slightly different coverage.

The final point as regards coverage is one that has already been mentioned. We should like to emphasize that the present review deals largely with particular types of personal income. The review on *Personal Incomes* [B 34] by T. Stark covers the broader subject of personal income as one entity. This review examines some constituent parts of the total at the individual level; namely, wage rates and salary scales, and earnings.

1.3. Plan of the Review

The way in which the various concepts of income which are discussed in this volume are linked together is shown in the accompanying diagram (see page 13), which gives an outline plan of the review.

The review starts with chapters on wage rates (Chapter 2) and salary scales (Chapter 3). These are the most basic elements of pay. When other payments above the basic rates or scales, including overtime, bonus, shift, and other premium payments, are added to these, one arrives at total earnings, which are the subject of Chapters 4 and 5.

Chapter 6 deals with fringe benefits and labour costs, whilst Chapter 7 deals with historical data on earnings and its components.

Finally, in Chapter 8 we evaluate the various statistical sources—for coverage, reliability, and availability—and end with a few recommendations. But before we start to describe the statistical sources for these various concepts we shall first review other source books which cover some of the same ground.

1.4. Other Source Books

There have been earlier descriptions of wages and earnings statistics that are worth mentioning at the outset. They are generally rather out of date but at least give a good picture of the historical statistics. In Kendall's *Sources and Nature of the Statistics of the United Kingdom, Volume 1* [B 23], which was published in 1952, there was a chapter on Labour Statistics by Ralph B. Ainsworth (the Director of Statistics at the Ministry of Labour). This described statistics of employment, unemployment, working population, wages and hours, and retail prices. The section on wages and hours is less than three pages long, but the main official sources are described together with a record of when each enquiry was started (or stopped). That source is useful for a researcher trying to obtain information on historical wages and earnings data; but it gives little information on post-war data because it is of course now over twenty-five years out of date.

In 1958 a revised edition of *Guides to Official Sources; No. 1. Labour Statistics* [B 39] was published by the Interdepartmental Committee on Social and Economic Research which had been set up by the Government. This enlarged and updated an earlier version which had been published in 1948 [B 38]. The relevant sections of this new official guide

PLAN OF THE REVIEW

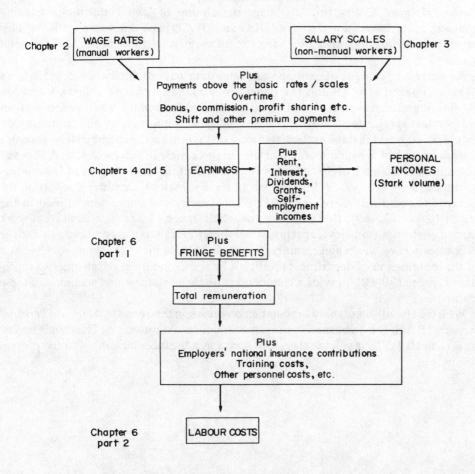

were Chapter 5 on Statistics of Wage Rates, Normal Hours of Work, and Other Conditions of Employment, and Chapter 6 on Statistics of Earnings and Actual Hours Worked. Together these two chapters describe, in some twelve pages, all the official sources on wage rates and earnings, including most of the official series dating back to the nineteenth century and references to official enquiries and reports on pay matters. A less comprehensive official guide, which presents a check-list of the main official sources, is given in the Central Statistical Office's *Guide to Official Statistics* [B 40], first published in 1976 and revised in 1978. A description of the statistics which existed in 1968, plus a guide to some of the earlier series, was given in the *British Labour Statistics; Historical Abstract 1886–1968* [QRL 18], which was published by the Department of Employment in 1971 (see Section 7.3).

Devons' *British Economic Statistics* [B 7], published in 1958, contained a chapter on Incomes (Chapter VIII). This surveyed the current and past indices of wage rates, the statistics on what he called 'wage earnings' (by which he meant the earnings of manual workers), a similar section on 'salary-rates', and sections on other incomes and the distribution of incomes. Harvey's *Sources of Statistics* [B 21], the second edition of which was published in 1969, also contained a separate chapter on Labour (Chapter Five). This gave a very brief five-page description of labour statistics, including information on international sources (ILO and OECD) and American statistics. This survey is far from comprehensive, however, although it might be of use to the general reader.

An interesting critique of existing wage rates data was provided in 1965 in Layton's 'Wages—Fog or Facts?' [B 26]. This paper reviewed the existing published information on wages and conditions of work and concluded that what was needed was an independent service for the collection and analysis of information on incomes. (One should perhaps add that the author later went on to form such an organization, Incomes Data Services Ltd, which is mentioned later in this review in Section 2.4.1.) A very full description of the work of the Statistics Department of the then Ministry of Labour was published in the next year (1966) as part of the Estimates Committee's report on the *Government Statistical Services* [B 41]. The Ministry's evidence was printed in the report (pages 122–69); this reviewed the whole range of statistical collection work carried out by the Statistics Department and therefore acts as a most useful guide to the official sources on wages and earnings statistics as of that time. The Minutes of Evidence of the examination of departmental officials by the Committee, which are also reproduced (pages 170–90), provide a commentary on the usefulness and adequacy of these statistics.

We have already mentioned the companion review in this series by Stark, on *Personal Incomes* [B 34]. It is published in the same volume as Atkinson and Harrison's review on *Wealth* [B 1]. That volume therefore serves as a useful complement to the present review.

CHAPTER 2

WAGE RATES

2.1. Introduction

Wage rates are the basic rates of pay for the standard duties of manual workers. Most of the official information on wage rates refers to the minimum entitlements of workers subject to centrally determined collective agreements or statutory orders. In the case of many such agreements and orders no worker may actually receive just these minimum entitlements. But these wage rates provide an indication of what the standard minimum rate of pay is for a specified working week of 'normal' hours. The term is usually used to refer to manual workers but is also applied to some occupations, such as shop-assistants, which are normally classified as non-manual.

In many industries voluntary agreements are regularly made between representatives of employers and employees about wage rates and other conditions of employment. These wage rates are the agreed basic wages for manual workers fixed in national agreements. National collective agreements between employers or employers' associations and trade unions now cover something like 9,000,000, mostly manual, workers.

These agreements have gradually developed since the middle of the nineteenth century. In some industries, however, where strong unions did not exist and where voluntary negotiating procedures did not develop to the same extent, the State has stepped in to set up statutory bodies which have the specific duties of setting minimum rates of wages. These Wages Councils are responsible for setting minimum rates of wages for about 3,000,000 workers. So altogether something like 12,000,000 workers are covered by Wages Councils or national collective agreements although there is some overlap between the two. Even more workers are 'affected by' national agreements, i.e. they follow the national agreements but are not directly covered by them (see Elliott and Steele [B 15]). The vast majority of manual workers are therefore affected by these agreements. The rates of pay which are set by these bodies are usually minimum entitlements or standard rates of wages for specified groups of workers. Generally these wage rates will be much less than the actual earnings of the workers involved because first, average rates of wages actually paid are usually greater than the minima, and, secondly, because earnings also include other payments such as overtime, bonuses, and merit awards. But it is these minima which are used to calculate indices of wage rates.

An annual listing of wage rates is given in the Department of Employment's publication *Time Rates of Wages and Hours of Work* [QRL 81]. This lists details of virtually all the national collective agreements and Wages Orders for a particular time in each year, generally April.

To keep this volume up-to-date changes in wage rates are published monthly by the Department of Employment in a small leaflet entitled *Changes in Rates of Wages and*

Hours of Work [QRL 21]. The most important changes each month are also reported in the Monthly Statistics section of the *Department of Employment Gazette* [QRL 24] under the heading 'Basic rates of wages and normal hours of work'. Finally, indices of weekly and hourly wage rates are published in the statistical series section of the *Gazette* in Table 131. All of these publications will be referred to again and will be discussed in more detail below.

For a moment we return to the coverage of these nationally bargained rates of wages. The number of workers covered by each of the principal national collective agreements was first listed by the Department of Employment following a survey which it carried out in 1973 (*Gazette,* November 1973, page 1151, reproduced in Appendix A). In the survey, information was sought from the parties to about 300 national collective agreements. Most of the agreements surveyed covered manual workers and groups such as shop workers, and the police, fire, and prison services. Finding out how many workers are covered by an agreement is a more difficult task than it might appear. In some cases, where there are few employers involved, it is possible to estimate the numbers of workers covered. But if there are a large number of small firms party to the agreement then the problem becomes much more difficult. There are also cases where workers are affected by more than one agreement. This is particularly common where the demarcation between different jobs or occupations is not clear, and it also occurs when there is an overlap between a national collective agreement and a Wages Order. For these reasons the Department emphasizes that the figures for the numbers covered by national agreements are necessarily only broad estimates. Workers who are nominally covered by a national agreement may be paid at higher rates since the national agreement often sets only the standard minima. Also, workers in firms which are not themselves parties to the agreement may be indirectly affected by the terms of that agreement. The numbers covered will be subject to change over time as industries or occupations expand or contract. From time to time, therefore, rather large changes in the estimates of numbers covered by an agreement may appear, but they generally reflect a catching-up of information rather than a sudden annual change.

Since 1974 a list of the numbers of workers covered by principal national collective agreements in the United Kingdom has appeared each year in an Appendix to *Time Rates of Wages and Hours of Work* [QRL 81]. These lists, based originally on the 1973 survey, contain the latest estimates of numbers covered given by the negotiating parties. But since the numbers covered are sometimes not known accurately by the parties to the agreements, these figures must be treated with caution.

The same difficulties arise in estimating the numbers covered by Wages Councils. The number of Wages Councils is gradually being reduced since there has been a general policy over a number of years to encourage the setting up of voluntary collective bargaining machinery to replace statutory wage regulation. Wages Councils had initially been set up where the organization of workers was too weak for voluntary bargaining to work. The first statutory regulation of wages came in 1909 with the Trade Boards Act. The Act was originally intended to provide for statutory minimum wages in 'sweat-shops' and four Trade Boards were originally set up. However, the Act was extended in 1918 to other areas where 'no adequate machinery exists for the effective regulation of wages throughout the trade' (see E. Wigham's *Strikes and the Government* [B 36]). In the next three years a further thirty-seven new boards were established, extending the number of workers protected by statutory regulation to 1,500,000. By the end of the Second World War the Trade Board system had been extended into retail distribution and catering and there were fifty-seven Trade Boards, now renamed Wages Councils. For the next twenty-five years the number of Wages Councils fluctuated very little but in the 1970s their number began to decline. Thus in 1975, for instance, the number of councils fell from forty-nine to forty-five, their coverage falling from 3,250,000 to 3,000,000 workers (*Gazette* [QRL 24], May 1976, page 488). The present powers of Wages Councils are defined by the Wages Councils Act 1959 (as amended by the Employment Protection Act 1975) which gives the councils independent status with membership consisting of equal numbers of employers' and workers' representatives and three independent members, being appointed by the Secretary of State for Employment. The councils' proposals on minimum terms and conditions are effected by Wages Orders and are enforced by the Wages Inspectorate (see 'The wages inspector cometh', *Gazette* [QRL 24], February 1977). Full details of the Wages Orders can only be found in the Orders themselves, available from HMSO, but much of the information is given in *Time Rates of Wages and Hours of Work* [QRL 81] which also includes a summary table on 'Industries covered by Wages Orders'. For a history of the Wages Councils, see Guillebaud's *The Wages Council System in Great Britain* [B 18] and Bayliss' *British Wages Councils* [B 2].

There are also three Agricultural Wages Boards set up under the Agricultural Wages Acts. These three boards, for England and Wales, Scotland and Northern Ireland, operate in the same way as the Wages Councils in prescribing weekly minimum wages, standard working hours, holidays, and other conditions of employment. They also examine and value payments-in-kind which can be reckoned as a part-payment of wages. Agricultural earnings in general are reviewed in Section 5.2.4.

The total of 12,000,000 workers covered by national collective agreements, Wage Councils, and the Agricultural Wages Boards, represents as much as 80–90 per cent of all manual workers. Information on the terms and conditions of these agreements is collected by the Department of Employment and is then recorded in the various publications already mentioned. Details of agreements are mostly obtained on a voluntary basis from the negotiating parties.

2.2. Official Sources of Wage Rates

Information on wage rates is published by the Department of Employment, yearly in the annual volume *Time Rates of Wages and Hours of Work* [QRL 81] and monthly in *Changes in Rates of Wages and Hours of Work* [QRL 21] and the *Gazette* [QRL 24]. We now examine these three sources in turn.

2.2.1. *Time Rates of Wages and Hours of Work* [QRL 81]

This annual publication presents a 'stock-take' of existing collective agreements for April in each year. In theory one should be able to produce this volume by taking the previous year's issue and revising it according to the information on changes in wage rates provided by the monthly leaflet. In practice this may prove a little difficult because the annual volume gives a rather more comprehensive description of the national agreements, albeit a static view, than that provided by the report on monthly changes.

The first handbook on wage rates was published in 1893, in the first year of the Labour Department of the Board of Trade. A series, originally called *Standard Time Rates* [QRL 72], later published with its present longer title, has been published regularly since then. From 1946 onwards, with one exception in 1953, the series has been published annually with a publication lag of less than six months. Up to 1952 the annual volume referred to the position in about September each year. But in 1954 the date was changed to 1st April and then, from 1972, to the month of April. Full details of something like 280 agreements and Wages Orders, covering mainly manual workers, are reported. The source of the information is given in each case with the date from which the agreement became operative. Particulars of the minimum time rates or remuneration for adult workers are given together with information on the normal hours of work, shift-work, overtime premiums, basic rates for piece-workers, guaranteed week arrangements, and methods of work grading. In short, all the standards terms and conditions of service are listed.

In addition further material on particular topics is collated at the back of each volume. There is a table, already mentioned in Section 2.1, on 'Industries covered by Wages Orders'. For each group listed in the table the general minimum time rate for adults and the normal weekly hours for the April in question are recorded. There is also a cross-reference to the fuller details given earlier in the volume. The Wages Councils and Boards for Northern Ireland are listed separately from those for Great Britain, although the information in the main part of the volume refers to the whole of the United Kingdom unless it is stated otherwise. Then there are appendices on young workers, overtime rates of pay, holidays with pay, and the numbers of workers covered by agreements. As already indicated the only further material on wage rates is that contained in the Wages Orders and copies of the original collective agreements; the latter are generally not available. But we should emphasize again that the wage rates reported are generally minimum rates only and that the rates actually paid may differ from the national rates for a whole variety of reasons. On average the difference between nationally and locally negotiated wage rates has been calculated by Elliott and Steele [B 15] as being less than 5 per cent of 'standard weekly earnings', though this is a controversial finding (see Brown and Terry [B 3]). While some company agreements are monitored by the Department of Employment they are generally neither reported in the *Gazette* [QRL 24] nor used in compiling the wage rates index.

2.2.2. *Changes in Rates of Wages and Hours of Work* [QRL 21]

This monthly leaflet reports the latest changes in the basic rates of wages or minimum entitlements and the normal hours of work of manual workers covered by national agreements and statutory wage orders, and therefore updates the annual volume through the year. These changes give the most up-to-date official information on what is happening in national wage settlements. The reporting and publication lag is little more than a month; for instance, the January issue, which covers all the national settlements reported for the period up to the end of December, is issued at the end of January.

Settlements which have been reported belatedly or have been backdated to an earlier month are recorded alongside the most recent settlements.

The following information on wage rates is recorded:

Industry: e.g. Baking.

District: e.g. England and Wales.

Date from which change took effect: e.g. 28 November 1976.

Classes of workers: e.g. workers employed by Co-operative Societies.

Particulars of change: e.g. amount of increase for adults, juveniles, part-time workers, etc., overtime rates, London allowance, and other terms and conditions of employment.

Changes which have resulted from statutory Wages Orders and second or other stages of long-term agreements are footnoted. The number of workers affected by changes reported in the month and estimates of the total amount of the increases resulting are also published although the caveat that 'this does not necessarily imply a corresponding change in "market" rates or actual earnings' is always entered. A breakdown of the total increase between national agreements, Wage Orders, and other sources (e.g. index linking) is also made. Finally, two tables are published. Table (a) shows the approximate numbers affected by increases, and the estimated amount of increase in basic weekly entitlements arising from changes in wage rates during the current year, by industry group and in total, with the total figures for the corresponding period of the previous year entered below. Table (b) shows the month by month effect of changes over the most recent thirteen-month period, indicating the number of workers affected each month and the estimated amount of increase in the total of the national wage rates bill.

The pay information reported is usually the change in rates in £ and p and the new level. One can therefore calculate percentage changes although it is sometimes necessary to go back to the annual volume to find the previous levels of rates and hours of work in order to understand fully the implication of the changes. For this purpose a cross-reference to the annual volume is given for all the relevant agreements mentioned.

This leaflet was first issued in 1966 and has been published each month since then with the exception of September 1966 to January 1967 and January to March 1973 when pay freezes meant that no changes were reported. Before 1966 the lists of changes were published in the *Gazette*. As we shall now see a summary of the main changes is still included in the *Gazette* each month.

2.2.3. *Wage rates in the* Gazette [QRL 24]

There are three sources of information on wage rates in the *Gazette*. The index of wage rates is dealt with separately in the next section (2.3). The other sources are first, the monthly report on the latest changes in wage rates and, secondly, the annual summary of the main changes during the previous year published in the January issue.

The monthly report on the latest changes in wage rates appears in the Monthly Statistics section of the *Gazette*. This is a short summary of the settlements reported in *Changes in Rates of Wages and Hours of Work* [QRL 21]. Since it appears in the *Gazette* it may be more readily accessible to non-specialists than the fuller publication. The settlements reported are the more important ones made during the month. Information on the number of workers covered by all the settlements reported in the month is recorded, as well as the aggregate increases in basic weekly entitlements involved.

Tables (*a*) and (*b*), as already described, are also reproduced. For most purposes, therefore, the monthly report in the *Gazette* is an adequate summary of *Changes in Rates of Wages and Hours of Work* [QRL 21]. Most researchers will find that the *Gazette*, plus perhaps the annual volume, meets most of their needs, although it only gives the details of the more important settlements each month.

The second source on wage rates in the *Gazette* is an annual article in the January issue, 'Rates of wages and hours of work in . . .'. This article shows movements in the wage rates index each month over the previous year and percentage changes in the index during each year in the last twenty years. But the main information is a table of all the more important settlements which occurred in the previous year, listed chronologically by date of agreement. The operative date and the brief details of changes are shown and there is also a listing of agreements made in the previous year which became effective or had stages in the year in question. The usual monthly table of the number of workers affected by increases and the total amount of increase in basic weekly entitlements, by industry, during the previous twelve months, is given in this article rather than in the Monthly Statistics section, as is the month by month account of the effect of changes. A long series of annual figures dating back to 1956 on the numbers affected by increases and the total amount involved is also given. Finally, there is also a section on developments in wage bargaining (e.g. the effect of incomes policies) during the past year. This annual article therefore gives a fairly full review of developments in nationally agreed wage rates over the previous year, but also gives a longer term perspective to movements in wage rates. In 1979 the article appeared in the May issue of the *Gazette*, rather than January, because of a large number of backdated settlements.

2.2.4. *Other official sources of wage rates*

A very useful alternative source of information on wage rates is the *British Labour Statistics Yearbook* [QRL 19], which has been published for each year since 1969. Each yearbook has included in Table 1 a list of the basic weekly wage rates for men in each of around seventy major national agreements or statutory orders, for a run of three or four years. Within each group the rates for the major occupations or skills are given. Since these figures are available in one table this is a useful source for scanning the data fairly quickly. For all the details other than weekly wages rates—for example, details of hours or of overtime rates—one must refer to the more voluminous sources already discussed. A similar table of rates for women in the major agreements was provided (Table 2), but since 1977 these tables have been integrated now that separate rates for men and women no longer exist.

The number of workers affected by changes in wage rates and the estimated net amounts of increase for different industrial groupings are set out in a further table annually for ten years, monthly for two years. For a long run of monthly or quarterly data one obviously needs a series of successive yearbooks and possibly the *Historical Abstract* [QRL 18] which gives details for the period up to 1968 (see Chapter 7 for a review of the historical data).

The other table of some interest which appears in the yearbooks and in the annual *Gazette* articles is a table on the methods by which increases in basic weekly wage rates have been achieved. Figures for ten years are shown. Direct negotiation and joint industrial councils and other voluntary bodies are generally responsible for at least 80 per cent of the total amount of increases. The remaining amount is largely achieved through the Wages Councils since arbitration is not very significant and sliding-scale agreements, which accounted for up to 10 per cent of total increases in the mid 1960s, now account for a negligible amount of the increase (apart from the 'thresholds' in 1974–5).

2.3. Monthly Index of Wage Rates

For over a hundred years statisticians have been producing indices of wage rates of manual workers which combine together the details of wage rates in individual agreements into one aggregate index. The earliest indices, relating to a small selection of representative grades in a selection of industries, are discussed in Chapter 7 on historical data. Since the last war the rates used in compiling these indices have been confined to those quoted in the national agreements and Wages Orders which we have already discussed. In this section we first consider the compilation of the index and then discuss the sources where it is published and its coverage.

2.3.1. *Compilation of the wage rates index*

The current index of wage rates measures the average movement each month in the level of full-time basic rates of wages or minimum entitlements fixed by a selection of national agreements and Wages Orders compared with the level of 31 July 1972 which is taken as 100. These agreements are selected as being representative of all national agreements in the various industries and changes are regarded as indicators of changes in all the agreements in the respective industry groups. The present base of 31 July 1972 = 100 is arbitrarily chosen and merely reflects the fact that the index is periodically revised so that the weights never become too much out of date. The present series is the third in the post-war period, the previous base dates being June 1947 = 100 and 31 January 1956 = 100. The major revision entailed in the re-basing procedure is re-weighting of the series. For the moment we shall confine our discussion to the current index and its associated weights, a description of which is given in an article in the September 1972 *Gazette* [QRL 24] pages 796–7.

An important fact about the wage rates index is that it has fixed weights. The index therefore shows the effects of settlements on a given group of workers without taking account of changes in industrial structure. Because of this familiar weighting problem it is of course necessary to re-weight the index periodically so that the weights do not become out of date. Arguably the period between the 1956 and 1972 revisions of the index was too lengthy, since by 1972 the wage rates index was being calculated according to weights which reflected the importance of different groups some seventeen years earlier. This is one of the points made in a critique of the official wage rates index by Elliott and Dean [B 13].

The weights used for combining the index numbers for each industry are the estimated wage bills for manual workers for each industry group at some date close to the revised base date. In the case of the present index the wage bills for manual workers shown by the *New Earnings Survey* [QRL 55] of April 1970 were used as a basis to determine the relevant weights. For the previous (1956 based) index the wage bills were taken from the October 1955 earnings enquiry (see Section 4.4) and special *ad hoc* enquiries. The 1972 weights are shown for each industry group in Table 1. The weight for all manufacturing industries (SIC Orders III–XIX) is just over half the total weight. The only industry group which does not feature in the index is SIC Order XXIV, which is Insurance, Banking, Finance and Business Services, where there are few manual workers. From July 1978 SIC XIX, 'other manufacturing industries' was removed from the index following the demise of the rubber industry National Joint Industrial Council; the weight for the industry was reallocated proportionately to all the other manufacturing industries (*Gazette,* May 1978, page 584).

TABLE 1. *Weights for the index of basic weekly wage rates (1972 based index)*

Standard Industrial Classification Order	Industry group	Weight
I	Agriculture, forestry, fishing	210
II	Mining and quarrying	305
III	Food, drink, and tobacco	436
IV and V	Coal and petroleum products; chemicals and allied industries	283
VI to XII	Metal manufacture; mechanical, instrument, and electrical engineering; shipbuilding and marine engineering; vehicles; metal goods not elsewhere specified	2,840
XIII	Textiles	352
XIV	Leather, leather goods, and fur	28
XV	Clothing and footwear	209
XVI	Bricks, pottery, glass, cement, etc.	227
XVII	Timber, furniture, etc.	179
XVIII	Paper, printing, and publishing	387
XIX	Other manufacturing industries	197
XX	Construction	970
XXI	Gas, electricity, and water	209
XXII	Transport and communication	1,034
XXIII	Distributive trades	802
XXV	Professional and scientific services	382
XXVI	Miscellaneous services	576
XXVII	Public administration and defence	374
	Total, all industries and services	10,000
	Total manufacturing industries only (Orders III to XIX)	5,138

Note: Order XXIV Insurance, banking, finance, and business services is not represented.

Source: *Department of Employment Gazette* [QRL 24], Sept. 1972.

The revision of the weights for the index from time to time means that there are discontinuities in the series of index numbers at intervals. A broad measure of the movement in wage rates over a long period can, however, be made by linking the various series. This is possible because at each re-basing and re-weighting there is an overlap of one month covered at the end of the old series and at the start of the new series (e.g. July 1972). This procedure is of course not exact but it is a necessary compromise when a long series is required. The extent of error in adopting a linking procedure will of course depend on how far the constituent series tend to diverge over time. In general, movements in relative wages over time have not been large so that there is some empirical justification for linking series, although the user of a linked series should always point out that a discontinuity does exist. The *Gazette* [QRL 24] article of September 1972 gives an example of the effect of different weights on the wage rates index over the period 1956 to 1972. Taking January 1956 = 100 the weekly wage rates index for July 1972 was 248.9 using the new 1972 series weights and 249.3 using the old 1956 series weights. This difference of 0.2 per cent over sixteen and a half years is remarkably small and over shorter periods there were almost certainly greater divergences. The linking of the wage rates series should be done multiplicatively. Index numbers in the new series (July 1972 = 100) are multiplied by the corresponding index number for July 1972 in the old series (January 1956 = 100) and divided by 100 to derive an index number in terms of the old series. As an example, the 'all workers all industries and services' series can be converted from the 1972 to the 1956 base by multiplying the new index numbers by 249.5 and dividing by 100 (these being the appropriate index numbers for July 1972 for the old and new series). The similar link between the 1947 and 1956 series is 1.561 (see February 1957 *Gazette*, page 50).

2.3.2. *Information on the wage rates index*

The wages rates index is published each month in the *Gazette* [QRL 24], in the monthly statistics section and in Table 131 of the statistical series at the back. This table shows movements in the index over about twenty-four months, together with annual figures going back to the base year, for eighteen industry groups and for manufacturing industries and services combined. The figures given relate to all manual workers in the United Kingdom. Figures for basic weekly wage rates, normal weekly hours and basic hourly rates of wages are given. The latter series is derived from the two former ones. Of those two series the basic weekly wage rates index is the one that we have been discussing so far. The index of normal weekly hours is constructed in the same way as the weekly wage rates index from data on national agreements, etc., but in this case actual hours (not indices of hours) are combined using weights based on the estimated numbers of manual workers in the various industry groups (see *Gazette*, September 1972). In addition to the weekly wage rates index the hourly wage rates index is constructed to abstract from changes in the length of the normal working week. In the past, reductions in the normal hours of work have meant that the hourly series has often moved sharply ahead of the weekly series. However, in recent years normal hours have settled at forty per week in a large number of industries so that the two series have moved very closely together.

Until 1976 separate indices for men, women, and juveniles were published in Table 130 of the *Gazette*. These figures were shown just for the two main series—all industries and manufacturing industries, with details of weekly rates, normal hours, and hourly rates. It was of course a very useful source for examining, for instance, relative movements in male and female rates of pay. It is therefore unfortunate that these data are no longer published.

The reason why these separate series are no longer published is the need to conform to the Equal Pay Act of 1970 and the Sex Discrimination Act of 1975 (see January 1977 *Gazette* [QRL 24]). All agreements must now conform to this legislation, so it has become increasingly difficult, if not impossible, to distinguish between rates of pay for males and females from published data. It is, however, unfortunate that the separate data on juveniles will not be available, since the legislation has not affected this particular group, although adult rates are commonly paid at much lower ages than in the past.

The index of basic weekly wage rates provides an up-to-date indicator of what is happening to the national wage rates bill, that is the hypothetical amount that is paid out as basic wages to those covered by agreements. The index for January, for instance, relates to the last day in January and is published approximately one month later in the February *Gazette*. But the principal figures are first released in a Press Notice which is circulated less than three weeks after the date to which they refer. Because this is so soon after the event some settlements have still to be taken into account, in particular those with retrospective effect. Settlements which are concluded or reported subsequently are incorporated to give revised figures. But the reporting procedures are in general very good so that revisions are usually very small in their overall impact on the index, rarely amounting to more than one-half of one per cent except where large groups of workers settle retrospectively.

The major wage rate series are also recorded elsewhere. The *Monthly Digest of Statistics* [QRL 52] gives index numbers of basic wage rates and normal hours for all industries and services and for manufacturing industries, and the index numbers of basic weekly rates for each industrial group. Up to the end of 1976 the separate figures for men, women, and juveniles were given but, as with the *Gazette*, have now been discontinued. *Economic Trends* [QRL 27] also includes index numbers of basic weekly wage rates for all industries and for manufacturing, monthly for about fifteen months, quarterly for about six years and annually for ten years. Longer runs of quarterly and annual data for over twenty years are given in the *Economic Trends Annual Supplement* [QRL 28], published from 1975 onwards. Details of the wage rates index are also given each year in the *British Labour Statistics Yearbooks* [QRL 19], first published in 1969. Indeed details of nearly all the official series on wages and earnings are given in the yearbooks and supplement information given in the *British Labour Statistics; Historical Abstract 1886–1968* [QRL 18]. The disadvantage of the yearbooks, however, is that generally one can find data for only a few years so that one needs to look at several issues to establish a long time series.

The primary source for data on wage rates remains the *Gazette* [QRL 24], despite the numerous other sources where this information is reproduced.

2.4. Other Sources of Wage Rates

The wage rates material discussed in Section 2.2 refers only to nationally agreed rates. This material is the only official information on wage rates. In this section we first discuss other sources of information on wage rates and then mention the work at Aberdeen University where the official data have been processed on to a computer.

2.4.1. *Other wage rates information*

We have already mentioned that in many cases basic wage rates are decided as a result of company and plant bargaining and not by national agreements. The most important companies which are not parties to national agreements are in the motor industry and the chemical and petroleum industries (although information on wage rates in ICI is published by the Department). In these sectors the wage structure is largely determined by agreements in major companies such as Ford and Esso or in plant agreements which are rarely publicized. Information on these agreements is not reported officially so that a variety of other sources have to be used.

There are two private bodies which are involved in reporting on matters concerned with pay. These are Incomes Data Services (IDS) of 140 Great Portland Street, London W1, and Industrial Relations Services of 170 Finchley Road, London NW3. Both these organizations were set up in the mid 1960s to provide a service in reporting developments in the labour market. Each produces a fortnightly report on the current situation; these are known respectively as *Incomes Data Report* [QRL 41] and *Industrial Relations Review and Report* [QRL 43]. Both of these are available to subscribers only.

Incomes Data Reports [QRL 41] regularly record all the settlements that become known to the organization over the previous fortnight. The old rates, the new rates, and the amount of increase are usually reported for all the different grades and scales involved. The parties to the agreement are listed plus any other details on hours, shifts, overtime, allowances, holidays, etc. Where the settlement is notable for some reason a commentary is given. The reports deal not only with wage rates but also with earnings and all other matters of pay. An innovation in 1977 has been periodic articles on the pay of certain groups of workers, looking especially at concepts of real and net pay. The particular usefulness of these reports for wage rates information is that the Settlements section of each issue gives details of many of the more important plant and company agreements which are by their very nature excluded from the official reporting of the national agreements. IDS is therefore often the only readily available source, apart from occasional reporting in the Press, of many of these important non-national agreements. IDS also publishes a series of in-depth *Studies* [QRL 42] on particular pay topics. These are described in rather more detail in Section 3.2.2 on salaries. Many of these studies are concerned with wages of manual workers and provide useful information which is not available elsewhere.

Industrial Relations Review and Report [QRL 43], as its name implies, tends to be rather more concerned with the institutional and legal side of industrial relations. Although it reports particular settlements it does so rather irregularly and, apparently, only when there is a major issue at stake. It frequently reports on arbitration rulings or court proceedings in particular cases but does not give a comprehensive record of settlements in the same way as IDS. As a source of statistics it is therefore a less useful publication than *Incomes Data Reports* [QRL 41], but its coverage of industrial relations matters is far more comprehensive.

A certain amount of information on wage negotiations and wage settlements is reported in each issue of the *British Journal of Industrial Relations* [QRL 17]. This journal, published three times a year since it was started in 1963, always includes a Chronicle section for the four-month period preceding each issue. In this section there is a record of the most recent statistics, government policy, the activities of trade unions and employers, and negotiations and agreements. Under the last topic it is only major settlements or disputes which tend to be mentioned, so the coverage is rather scanty. Whilst one could not therefore rely on the Chronicle as a record of settlements in the recent period it does at least give some indication of what has happened in the major agreements.

Two other sources of wage rates statistics which have been used by researchers but which also have a scanty coverage are *Labour Research* [QRL 48] and the *TGWU Handbook* [QRL 80]. The former, the monthly publication of the Labour Research Department (a research body financed by trade unions, trades councils, and constituency Labour parties), was used by Knowles and Thorne in their 1961 article on 'Wage rounds 1948–1959' [B 25]. The Labour Research Department was originally founded by the Fabians and has produced its monthly report ever since 1917. The Industrial Notes section of that publication gives a summary of current wage claims and settlements and reports on the progress of current disputes. Knowles and Thorne used the information on some 130 negotiating groups over the period 1948–59. But only 530 settlements are recorded in that period, implying that many of the settlements for each group are excluded, and the total number of groups is far from comprehensive. The coverage is clearly unsatisfactory and inevitably patchy since it relies on reporting in the Press and private contacts.

The *TGWU Handbook* [QRL 80], the handbook of the Transport and General Workers' Union, was used by Knowles and Robinson in their 1962 article 'Wage rounds and wage policy' [B 24]. It was introduced in 1952 in a loose-leaf binder form for the use of union officials. Updates to the information contained in it were issued at regular intervals until it was discontinued in 1965. It recorded settlements for about 175 negotiating groups in which the union had an interest, but suffered from the disadvantage that all other settlements were excluded. The information given included the minimum time-rates and conditions of service for male and female adults and juveniles in the lowest paid groups in a number of industries in which the TGWU had an interest. For all the groups listed, the current rate was given, together with all past rates going back to June 1947. The advantage of this publication compared with the official publication, although it was far from comprehensive, was that it gave the history of the rates and increases for a period of years on one sheet, whereas users of the official publications have to look through a large number of annual volumes of *Time Rates of Wages and Hours of Work* [QRL 81] in order to find the same information. The other information provided related to working hours, shift work, overtime, holidays, piecework, and the guaranteed week. A large supplement appeared from 1953 onwards on road haulage workers in about sixty-five different organizations, a particular concern of the union. But neither the *TGWU Handbook* nor *Labour Research* were at all comprehensive though each provides some information which is not available in the official coverage.

A most useful source of information on earnings in specific occupations are the *Reports of the National Board for Prices and Incomes* [QRL 61] published between 1966 and 1971. During this period the Board issued 170 reports on a whole variety of topics concerned with pay and prices. These reports are listed and summarized in the *Fifth and Final General Report* [QRL 32] and its supplement (see Appendix B). About fifty of the reports are specifically concerned with the pay and conditions of manual workers. These give information on wage rates and earnings. Much of this work involved new survey work but they are useful anyway as a source of reference for investigators in the different areas covered. These reports are mentioned again in Section 3.3.1, where the information on salaries provided by the reports is discussed.

From time to time there have also been enquiries of an *ad hoc* nature such as the 1974 Pay Board *Special Report on the Relative Pay of Mineworkers* [B 43] and the 1974 Halsbury *Report of the Committee of Inquiry into the Pay and Related Conditions of Service of Nurses and Midwives* [B 19]. Both of these contain useful material in statistical appendices. The *Reports of the Royal Commission on the Distribution of Income and Wealth* [QRL 64] are also beginning to present much useful information on pay, although most of this has so far been concerned with income distribution and higher pay (see Section 3.3.3).

2.4.2. *Aberdeen wage rates database*

The official wage rates data collected by the Department of Employment have already been fully described in Section 2.2. These are available monthly in the *Gazette* [QRL 24] and *Changes in Rates of Wages and Hours of Work* [QRL 21], and annually in *Time Rates of Wages and Hours of Work* [QRL 81] and the *British Labour Statistics Yearbooks* [QRL 19]. In addition, a series of annual figures from 1947 to 1968 is given for each of the major bargaining groups in the *British Labour Statistics; Historical Abstract* [QRL 18]. But all this material is presented in a rather indigestible form. Apart from the last source, much painstaking research is necessary in order to extract information for any particular group over a period of years. Fortunately, however, the official material has been extracted and processed by researchers at the University of Aberdeen. The information has been established in a database and now, linked with other information, it provides a comprehensive structuring of the principal details of all major national wage settlements over the period since 1950.

The major work involved in constructing the database was carried out during 1973 and 1974 at the University of Aberdeen by R. F. Elliott and R. Steele of the Department of Political Economy and D. M. R. Bell of the Computing Centre. A description of the data and the means of accessing it is contained in Elliott and Bell's 'Wage rates database' [B 12].

The principal information contained in the Aberdeen database refers to manual workers and is taken from the official information contained in *Time Rates of Wages and Hours of Work* [QRL 81] and *Changes in Rates of Wages and Hours of Work* [QRL 21]. Further information on the coverage of, and parties to, the national agreements was obtained from unpublished Department of Employment sources. Details of all the wage settlements of the 190 largest national negotiating groups are recorded for the period since 1950. All those negotiating groups which covered 5,000 or more workers over all or part of the period were selected for analysis from a total of 280 groups covered at some time over the period in the official statistics. For each of these 190 negotiating groups the following basic details are recorded:

1. The title of the negotiating group.
2. The main SIC Order (1968 classification).
3. The bargaining system in 1950 and in 1973 according to the following classification:
   (1) Wages Council/Board.
   (2) Whitley Council.
   (3) Public corporation/nationalized industry.

    (4) Local authority.
    (5) Private employer.
    (6) Other.
4. The principal trade unions involved (up to four, with the relevant operative years specified).
5. The geographical area covered in 1950 and in 1973 according to the following classification:
    (1) GB or UK—single national settlement.
    (2) GB or UK—settlement with district variation.
    (3) E or E & W or E & W & NI—single national settlement.
    (4) E or E & W or E & W & NI—settlement with district variation.
    (5) Scotland.
    (6) Northern Ireland.
    (7) Local agreement.
6. Approximate numbers of workers covered—in 1950, 1955, 1960, 1965, 1970 and 1972.
7. Wage rate as percentage of standard weekly earnings as given by one of the following specified sources:
    (1) NES 1970 agreement.
    (2) NES 1970 MLH.
    (3) NES 1970 SIC Order.
    (4) NES1970 occupation.
    (5) NES 1968 agreement.
    (6) NES 1968 MLH.
    (7) Other source

For each negotiating group there are then a number of settlement occurrences, each giving the full particulars of one settlement (the number of occurrences for each negotiating group varying with the frequency of settlement). The information recorded for each of these settlements is as follows:

1. The title of the negotiating group.
2. A chronologically allocated settlement number.
3. The date of implementation—year and week.
4. The date of settlement—year and week.
5. The standard weekly hours.
6. Whether the time rate or minimum earnings level is recorded.
7. The basic weekly and hourly rates (including standard supplements) for the following four representative grades:
    (1) Top male (the highest-paid skilled occupation).
    (2) Semi-skilled male (selected after consultation with members of the negotiating group).
    (3) Bottom male (the basic labouring grade).
    (4) Semi-skilled female (selection similar to semi-skilled male).
8. The form of arbitration or government intervention, if any, under the following classification:
    (1) National Arbitration Tribunal or Industrial Disputes Tribunal.
    (2) Industrial Court or Industrial Arbitration Board.

(3) Court of Inquiry.

(4) *Ad hoc* arbitration Board or single arbitrator.

(5) Public sector Arbitration Board.

(6) Committee of Inquiry and Investigation.

(7) National Board for Prices and Incomes.

(8) Other forms of intervention.

9. Whether it is a long-term or staged settlement.

10. Whether or not a cost of living clause operates.

The definition of a settlement is important, in particular with respect to detail 9 described immediately above. When settlements are in different calendar years then they are treated as separate settlements, even if resulting from one set of negotiations. When more than one settlement occurs in the same calendar year, but they are the result of separate sets of negotiations, they are also treated as separate settlements. However, if more than one settlement is implemented within the same calendar year but they are the result of the same set of negotiations, then they are treated as part of one settlement. In this case the settlements are aggregated to the last implementation date in that year. This is an arbitrary procedure but one that is necessitated by the complications involved in analysing and recording staged settlements.

Where different rates are given for different districts in the same negotiating group, the rule employed at Aberdeen has been to take the rate of the district with the highest rates, excluding London. Where one group of workers (e.g. top skilled grade) receives an increase but the others do not, then only the rate which changes is recorded. The implementation date is the date from which the new rates become payable and may be before or after the settlement date, which is the date when negotiations are concluded. Backdating is thus allowed for. Where cost of living clauses apply, the last implementation date in the calendar year is recorded, as with staged increases. A change in standard weekly hours with no change in wage rates is treated as a separate settlement, and the new hourly rates are computed.

In addition to this information on the agreements and settlements, details of price movements over the period since 1950 are also recorded. Movements in the following four retail price indices, taken from the *Gazette* [QRL 24], are used; all items, food, all items except food, and all items except seasonal food indices. These price data are fed in so that data on changes in *real* wage rates can be extracted if required. However, the retail price index relates to expenditure out of take-home pay (not gross pay) so that real increases should strictly be calculated for take-home pay.

The most important feature of the work at Aberdeen has been the structuring of the information detailed above in the computer database. As an initial step the raw information on wage levels is automatically processed in order to calculate the size of settlement producing the new basic weekly or hourly rates. The size of settlement is calculated and recorded in both percentage and absolute terms and crude and annual measures of each are computed. The crude measure merely expresses the size of the settlement as an increase over the previous wage level, while the annual measure adjusts for the time between settlements.

The database permits interrogation of the data in a great number of ways. One might, for instance, select bargaining system 3 (see page 27) which would isolate the size of settlements for all nationalized industries and public corporations. Alternatively one might decide to look at the trade unions involved or the area covered. There are numerous permutations of this sort which are possible. They have been made possible by the flexibility which has been built into the Aberdeen database. Some examples of the ways in which the database can be used are contained in Elliott's 'The national wage round in the United Kingdom; a sceptical view' [B 10], 'Public sector wage movements, 1950–1973' [B 11], and 'The frequency of wage settlements' [B 8], and Elliott and Shelton's 'A wage settlements index for 1950–1975' [B 14].

The 'raw' information contained in the Aberdeen wage rates database is available in Department of Employment publications. But now that the information has been computerized it is possible to handle the data very easily. The database has been deposited with the Social Science Research Council Survey Archive at Essex University and is thus available to all researchers.

CHAPTER 3

SALARY SCALES

3.1. Introduction

The term salaries is used to describe the earnings of white-collar workers. The fine dividing line between these workers and others is described in Section 1.1. In this section, however, we shall be dealing with salary scales, that basic payment for fixed duties which forms the major part of salaries. We deliberately use the word 'scales', in contrast to rates, because the non-manual worker can often advance along a given incremental scale; such a progression is most unusual for manual workers. Generally-speaking the information available on salary scales is much less extensive than that on wage rates (Chapter 2) or on earnings data in general (Chapter 4). We shall leave discussion of statistics on salaries, as opposed to salary scales which are discussed here, to the next Chapter on earnings.

Since the official sources on salary scales are not as good as those for wage rates and earnings, much of the information on them comes from unofficial sources. Although it is possible to obtain information on salary structures in public sector organizations, officially published sources of information are rather mixed and varied. In Section 3.3 below we mention official sources such as Review Body reports, the National Board for Prices and Incomes reports, and reports of *ad hoc* enquiries. However, we shall first look at the unofficial sources of salary statistics since these tend to cover a wider area than the official sources.

3.2. Unofficial Statistics on Salary Scales

Unofficial or non-governmental sources of statistics on salary scales are various and very mixed in quality. The coverage of salary scales is generally good in the public sector but very poor in the private sector. There are two reasons for this; first, fixed salary structures are more common in the public sector (and probably in large organizations generally), and secondly, there is greater availability of information on salary scales in the public sector than in the private sector, where disclosure is not so common. Nevertheless even obtaining information from the public sector is not easy since few published sources exist and time series are difficult to obtain. Researchers often have to deal directly with the organizations with which they are concerned and this can be a laborious and sometimes fruitless process. Certain information is available from salary surveys, which are discussed in Section 5.4. But the coverage of these surveys is often not exactly what is required, the samples used often change each year so that runs of data may be suspect, and the surveys are frequently not generally available and are expensive to purchase. Furthermore, these surveys rarely give details of actual salary

31

structures, usually confining themselves to average or median earnings which may prove difficult to interpret. Nevertheless, the problems of interpretation may also apply to salary scales since the quality of individuals employed in particular jobs (e.g. a clerk in the Civil Service) may change substantially over a period of years. However, there is one useful source of information on salary structures which is readily available, and this is the volume of statistics which has been compiled by the National and Local Government Officers Association (NALGO). We now go on to describe this (Section 3.2.1). We then examine the sources of salary scales data provided by Incomes Data Services (Section 3.2.2).

3.2.1. NALGO salaries data

For many years the research section at NALGO has been collecting information on salary scales in NALGO services and those outside services which it felt were most useful for comparative purposes. This material is provided by the trade unions in the organizations involved. The majority of the information is concerned with organizations in the public sector, the only exceptions being information for some of the major banks and insurance companies. As we have already mentioned, data for the private sector are much more difficult to obtain in the first place. Nevertheless, for the twenty-five to thirty groups involved the salaries information is extremely detailed and long runs of salary scales are available, in some cases going as far back as 1945. This is therefore the best source of data on salary scales that is presently available.

Information on scales for the period up to the end of 1967 is available in a single volume *Historical Salaries for NALGO and Other Services* [QRL 38]. This is available from NALGO. Information since 31 December 1967 is provided on loose-leaf sheets which are published as new scales become known. Since 1967 several new groups have been included in the NALGO coverage and all the previous groups have been retained. A check-list of those groups included in the historical volume and its updates is given in Table 2 below. For most of the groups information is given for all the salary grades normally used, including incremental points on the salary scales and age scales where relevant. If possible, information has been provided going back to the inception of national scales or to 1945, whichever is the later. Although this sometimes means that there are some omissions in the series, especially for groups only included since 1967, the NALGO data are still by far the most useful source for data on salary scales in the post-war period.

3.2.2. Incomes Data Reports and Studies

Incomes Data Services (IDS) is a private firm which was set up in 1966 with the purpose of providing an information service on all matters concerned with incomes. The main output of the organization is produced in two fortnightly series, *Incomes Data Reports* [QRL 41] and *Incomes Data Studies* [QRL 42].

The fortnightly reports were started in 1966 at the time when the company was first set up. The reports are divided into three sections. The first is a Review section, which deals with the latest developments in all matters concerned with pay. These developments may be the full description of recent important settlements, interpretations of

TABLE 2. *Coverage of NALGO salary statistics*

Group	Major occupational groupings[1] covered	Earliest date	Page reference to Historical volume [QRL 38]
1. Historical volume			pages
Local Government (E & W)	15	1946	2–35
Local Government (Scotland)	4	1946	38–48
National Health Service	7	July 1948	50–104
Electricity supply	4	April 1948	106–16
Gas staffs	4	April 1950	118–24
British Waterways	3	February 1949	126–9
Water Boards and Companies[2]	1	April 1966	130
New Towns	3	January 1956	132–5
Industrial Estates	3	August 1963	136–7
Transport[3]	4	May 1960	138–9
Port of London Authority	2	October 1946	140–3
Banks[4]	1	1946	146–52
BBC	2	August 1946	154–9
British Railways	1	July 1945	161–3
Civil Service	7	January 1947	164–79
National Coal Board	2	January 1951	180–2
Police	4	July 1949	183
Teachers	1	April 1945	184
2. Additional groups in updates			
British Airports Authority	4	January 1969	
BEA/BOAC	2	January 1968	
British Railways[5]	1	July 1968	
Fire Service	1	1967	
Insurance[6]	1	1968	
Metropolitan Water Board	6	1967	
Post Office	2	January 1970	
National Bus Company	3	February 1970	
Passenger Transport Executive		October 1974	
British Road Services[7]	6	September 1967	
London Transport	2	September 1968	
University Teachers	2	April 1966	
Water Boards[8]	1	August 1968	
Teachers[9]	1	1971	

Notes.

1. For example, clerical, professional, and technical; within each occupational grouping there may be several classes and then a scale of increments. The number of such occupational groupings understates the number of grades by about a factor of five.
2. Prior to April 1966, water industry staffs followed local government.
3. Scottish and Tilling Groups covered.
4. Clerical grades in Barclays, District, Lloyds, Martins, Midland, National Provincial, and Westminster Banks; information on Lloyds starts in 1946, in 1952 for others.
5. As from July 1968 management staffs covered; previously just clerical staff.
6. Clerical grades in Sun Alliance, Royal Exchange, Eagle Star, Provident Life, Pearl, and Prudential insurance companies.
7. After November 1971 also covers National Freight Corporation Management Staffs.
8. Water engineers covered from August 1968 in addition to general and supervisory grades.
9. As from 1971 Heads/Deputy Heads covered in addition to previous coverage of teachers.

incomes policy limits in particular cases, news about union changes, or other similar items. This section is generally preceded by a page on Key Points which is rather like an editorial.

The second section in each *Report* is a Settlements section. This lists the full details of some of the recent settlements, in single companies as well as in collective agreements. The numbers covered by these settlements varies from just a few hundred to hundreds of thousands. The coverage of settlements does not pretend to be comprehensive but the details given are extremely comprehensive. For most settlements the old and new rates for each occupation and grade are given, together with the cash and percentage increases which these suggest. Hours of work, holiday entitlements, shift payments, and other terms and conditions are listed where possible. Each year a full index to the *Reports*, both by settlement and by occupation, is produced. This enables one to trace the settlements for around 300 groups which are reported by Incomes Data Services each year. These settlements cover all types of worker, manual and non-manual. The reason for mentioning the IDS material here is that, whilst much of the information on manual workers' pay may be available elsewhere, the information on salary scales that IDS provides is often unique. The IDS *Reports* are a useful source for information on all types of earnings, but fill a particular gap in the salaries field.

The third section of each *Report* is an Intelligence section. This provides information on the latest official series on retail prices, average earnings, and basic weekly wage rates, plus a commentary on the latest developments in these statistics. It also reports on matters such as industrial tribunals, official publications on pay, and the latest issues of the IDS *Studies* series. A section on Overseas Information was replaced in 1975 by a supplementary service called *IDS International Report* [QRL 40] which covers developments in other, mainly European countries.

Incomes Data Studies [QRL 42] have also been published fortnightly since 1971. The *Studies* give a deeper analysis of particular groups of workers or of particular terms or conditions of service. Recent studies in the general field of salaries have been those on White Collar Allowances (IDS Study 115), Top Salaries (IDS Study 121), and Clerical Pay (IDS Study 141). The latter study may serve as an example. The pay of clerical workers in seventeen organizations is examined, five in the public sector and twelve in the private sector. A full description of the pay scales in each organization is given in a Record section which also includes details of the previous two pay scales. These figures are analysed to give summary information on differentials, allowances, increments, average pay increases, etc. Whilst such information is based on only a very small sample, the results are no worse than those which arise from salary surveys (Section 5.4). Indeed, a greater amount of independence may be present in these studies since IDS usually gives a very critical assessment of the material which it obtains. The *IDS Guide to Salary Surveys* [QRL 39] which will be mentioned in Section 5.4.1 is in fact part of the IDS studies series. The relevant issues of the IDS studies series for the Salary Guide are numbers 23 (1971), 63 (1973), 89 (1974), 112 (1975), 137 (1976), 161 (1977), and 185 (1978). Two previous salary guides were produced on a one-off basis in January 1969 and June 1970; the annual guides are published each January.

3.3. Official Statistics on Salary Scales

A certain amount of information on salary scales is provided by a variety of official sources, though none of these has as its prime function the provision of such statistics.

Furthermore, few of these other sources have much continuity since they have generally been the result of *ad hoc* enquiries rather than regular procedures. Also some of them, notably the *Reports of the National Board for Prices and Incomes* [QRL 61], may be regarded as being historical in nature and may therefore be of little interest to the current user of statistics. In the sections below we briefly mention each of these various sources.

3.3.1. *Reports of the National Board for Prices and Incomes* [QRL 61]

The reason for giving special mention to these reports, which were all issued in the period 1965–71, is that many of them were in-depth studies of the pay and conditions of particular groups of workers. A total of 170 reports were issued on topics concerned with pay, payments systems, costs, and prices. Of these about twenty reports were specifically concerned with salaries. A full listing of all the reports is given in Appendix B which is taken from the supplement to Report no. 170, the National Board for Prices and Incomes *Fifth and Final General Report* [QRL 32]. That last report also gives a summary of each of the 1970 reports and is therefore a useful reference book to the work of the Board.

The reports which specifically related to salary scales covered the following groups: white-collar staff in electricity supply (Report no. 5); Midland Bank Staff (6); the higher Civil Service (11); Scottish teachers' (15); General Accident staff (41); senior local government officers (45); solicitors (54, 134, and 164); Prudential and Pearl Assurance staff (74); gas staffs (86); BOAC pilots (88); employment agencies (89); university teachers (98 and 145); London Clearing Banks (106); top salaries in the private sector and nationalized industries (107); ICI staff (109); journalists (115); BICC staff (125); and senior officers in the Armed Forces (157). There was also a report on salary structures (132) as well as five general reports on successive periods of the Board's work.

Taken together these reports provide a substantial amount of information on salary scales although they tend to concentrate on earnings.

A later body, the Pay Board, which was in existence from 1972 to 1974, made very few specific investigations and therefore did not gather together the same amount of information as the earlier Board. One of its special reports covered the pay of scientists in the civil service—see Pay Board Advisory Report 3, *Civil Service Science Group* [QRL 56]—but the majority of its reports were of a general nature.

3.3.2. *Review Bodies, Royal Commissions, etc.*

Some information on salary scales is provided by reports of various Review Bodies and Royal Commissions. The former tend to issue annual reports and therefore give some continuity whilst the latter are usually single detailed reports following extensive investigations. From time to time there are also special committees of Inquiry which are set up to examine the pay of particular groups, usually in order to resolve a pay dispute.

The review bodies on Doctors' and Dentists' Remuneration and on Armed Forces Pay were both set up in 1971. The former was appointed in July 1971 '... to advise the Prime Minister on the remuneration of doctors and dentists taking any part in the

National Health Service' (see *Review Body on Doctors' and Dentists' Remuneration First Report* [QRL 63]). The latter, appointed in September 1971, had a similar remit—'. . . to advise the Prime Minister on the pay and allowances of members of Naval, Military and Air Forces of the Crown and of any women's service administered by the Defence Council' (see *Review Body on Armed Forces Pay First Report* [QRL 62]. The members of these review bodies, appointed by the Prime Minister, are supported by staff provided by the Office of Manpower Economics. Since 1971 they have issued reports at approximately one-year intervals. The usefulness of these reports as a source of salary statistics lies in the fact that they generally provide a full listing of the existing salary scales together with the scales recommended by the review body. Since the main criterion used has tended to be comparability with similar professions or the rest of the community, statistics illustrating these comparisons are sometimes given.

Doctors' and dentists' remuneration had previously been the subject of a Royal Commission from 1957 to 1960. The third and fourth chapters of the *Report* [QRL 67] dealt with the remuneration of doctors and dentists since 1948 and evidence about remuneration. From 1962 to 1970 a Review Body under Lord Kindersley made twelve reports on doctors' and dentists' pay. This was then superseded by the new Review Body in 1971.

The pay of the Armed Forces had also been the subject of six reports by the National Board for Prices and Incomes (see Section 3.3.1). The first of these reports had examined the method of pay determination for the Armed Forces—the Grigg formula of 1958 which simply tied the pay of officers to movements in civil service salaries. Later, a standing reference on the pay of the Armed Forces was set up, and from 1968 to 1970 five of these reports were issued, each of which contains a certain amount of information on pay scales in the Armed Forces.

The pay of teachers in schools, establishments of further education, and colleges of education was examined by a Committee of Inquiry appointed by the Secretary of State for Education and Science in 1974. This inquiry was chaired by Lord Houghton and gave a most detailed examination of the subject of teachers pay, since it was the first independent review of teachers' pay for thirty years. The *Report of the Committee of Inquiry into the Pay of non-University Teachers* [QRL 60] outlined the history of the background to the teachers' pay negotiations (paras. 6–14) and went on to compare teachers' pay with general movements in pay (paras. 42–6) and with that of other occupations (paras. 47–55). The pay structure in different schools—starting salaries, scales and increments, promotion prospects, and allowances—were all dealt with in great detail. But over half the report was taken up with a listing of the detailed recommendations and a large statistical appendix on the numbers of teachers and their earnings. In particular Section II of that appendix is concerned with the movements in the pay of teachers over the period 1964–74.

The Department of Education and Science also produces each year two reports on teachers' pay, *Scales of Salaries for Teachers in Primary and Secondary Schools, England and Wales* [QRL 69] and *Scales of Salaries for Teachers in Establishments of Further Education in England and Wales* [QRL 68]. These reports, which are the outcome of the Burnham negotiations, give the salary scales for all grades of teachers in all state-financed non-university teaching posts. Before the 1970s these reports were published at two- or even three-year intervals, depending on the frequency of settlements, but negotiations about new scales now take place annually and the reports are published every year.

A special article on teachers' pay appeared in the *Gazette* [QRL 24] in September 1976 (pages 963–8). This article was largely concerned with explaining differences between men's and women's earnings in the profession, but it gives some useful information on the earnings of different types of teacher for 1973.

A certain amount of information on teachers' pay is also available directly from the Department of Education and Science. In its annual series *Statistics of Education* [QRL 74], volume 4 on teachers regularly gives information on the salary scales and distribution of teachers by scales. One table gives the average salary and distribution of salary bands by type of school, sex, graduate status, and age of full-time teachers in maintained primary and secondary schools, while a second table gives the same sort of information for full-time teachers in grant-aided establishments of further education. These tables have been published every year since the series was started in 1961, so that there are now continuous figures for several years. The only complaint is that it takes the Department between two and three years to publish the figures so that the latest figures are always somewhat out of date.

In the year 1966/7 a special survey of qualified manpower was carried out in England and Wales by the General Register Office—now renamed the Office of Population Censuses and Surveys (OPCS). This was a sample survey following up some of the qualified people enumerated in the 1966 census. The results of this survey were published in the Statistics of Education series as special series 3, *Survey of Earnings of Qualified Manpower in England and Wales 1966–7* [QRL 77]. The detailed results are analysed by age, sex, subject of qualification, and occupation and provide a unique record of earnings by qualification.

Another review body which provides some useful information on salaries is the Top Salaries Review Board. This was set up in May 1971, originally with the task of examining the pay of Ministers and MPs. Its *First Report* [QRL 65] in December 1971 dealt with this subject at great length. But its main report so far was its sixth report *Report on Top Salaries* [QRL 65], which was published in December 1974. This report examined and recommended upon the pay of senior grades of the Higher Civil Service, senior officers of the Armed Forces, the Higher Judiciary, and chairmen and members of nationalized industry Boards. The current pay scales are listed (Appendix A) and the report includes an historical study (Appendix G) which analyses the salary structures of these groups in an historical context and considers the degree of interdependence between them. Two surveys by the Office of Manpower Economics are included; one is a survey of earnings at the Bar (Appendix K) and the other a survey of Top Salaries generally, including private industry (Appendix L).

Some of the material reported in the Review Body's Sixth Report, plus a lot of other material on top salaries, is used in an article by J. L. Fallick on 'The growth of top salaries in the post-war period' [B 16]. That article provides a useful guide to the available statistics on top salaries and also mentions some of the American literature on fringe benefits and total remuneration (which are looked at briefly in Chapter 6). It also refers to some of the recent work by the Royal Commission on Income Distribution and Wealth.

3.3.3. *Royal Commission on the Distribution of Income and Wealth*

The Royal Commission on the Distribution of Income and Wealth was appointed in August 1974 with a standing reference to analyse the 'current distribution of personal income and wealth and available information on past trends in that distribution which would cover personal incomes at all levels, earned income of all kinds, unearned income of all kinds, capital gains, and all forms of personal wealth'. This broad remit has already resulted in two major reports on the standing reference, *Report No. 1* [QRL 64] of July 1975 and *Report No. 4* [QRL 64] of October 1976. These reports have mainly been concerned with the distribution of income but are of interest in that they include some information from the DHSS and Inland Revenue which has been specially processed.

The Commission has also had special references on higher incomes (over £10,000 before tax) and low pay. Its report on higher incomes was published as Report No. 3, *Higher Incomes from Employment* [QRL 36] in January 1976. The present distribution and past trends of such incomes are examined (Chapter 2). There is a section devoted to managerial salaries and differentials in the UK and overseas (Chapter 3). This was supported by Background Paper No. 2, *Analysis of Managerial Remuneration in the United Kingdom and Overseas* [QRL 12], by Hay-MSL Limited, which looks at the UK, Australia, France, Germany, Canada, and the USA. There is a further section in the main report on fringe benefits and superannuation (Chapter 4) and one on salary determination at higher levels (Chapter 5). The information in this and other Royal Commission reports is frequently not original information, being taken from other official bodies or private sources, but the usefulness of the reports is that they draw the information together under one roof and provide a commentary upon it. The Royal Commission is gradually collecting together a most important body of work in the field of incomes and it is expected that future reports will continue to provide much useful information.

3.3.4. *Salary scales in the Civil Service and the Government*

Salary scales for most members of the Civil Service and for all members of the Government are given in the Civil Service Department's *Civil Service Yearbook* [QRL 23]. This has been published annually since 1974. It replaced a similar yearbook, *The British Imperial Calendar and Civil Service List* [QRL 16], which was first published in 1809 but only contained salary information from 1924 onwards. The information given in these volumes includes the salaries of the Civil Service and of members of the Government—the Prime Minister, members of the Cabinet, Ministers not in the Cabinet, Parliamentary Secretaries, Government Whips and the Law Officers. The maxima and minima of all the main salary scales in the general Civil Service are given, plus information on departmental classes (mainly specialist posts) and the Northern Ireland Civil Service. Figures for London weighting are given where relevant. The information generally relates to the position in the autumn of the preceding year; the 1977 yearbook, for instance, which was published early in 1977, relates to the salary scales obtaining at 30 September 1976. This source of salary scales, since it covers so many people and since it is published each year, is a most valuable source of information.

CHAPTER 4

EARNINGS—MAJOR OFFICIAL SOURCES

4.1. Introduction

The statistics on earnings generally relate to total gross payments in cash received by the individual from one employer. Payments in kind are sometimes included in earnings for three special groups; coal-miners, farm, and catering workers, but for all other groups payments in kind or fringe benefits are not considered as earnings but as part of 'total remuneration' (see Section 6.2). We have already indicated in the introduction (in Section 1.1 in particular) that the basic wage rate or salary scale is only one part, albeit the major part, of earnings. The make-up of pay is regularly surveyed in the *New Earnings Survey* (NES) [QRL 55], which is discussed below in Section 4.3. The April NES 1976, for instance, shows that about three-quarters of the pay of full-time manual men was made up of an element that approximates to basic pay. The figure is only approximate because the NES defines a category 'all other pay' which is equal to gross weekly earnings less overtime pay, payment by results, other incentive pay, and shift and other premium payments.

It is clear from the NES figures that the category of 'all other pay' forms a much higher proportion of earnings for non-manual workers than for manual, and for women than for men. This is largely because of the larger amount of paid overtime for manual and male workers generally and the greater importance of payment by results schemes for manual workers.

However, the category of 'all other pay' should not be equated with the basic wage rates examined in the previous chapter, which were minimum entitlements or standard rates as nationally agreed or as laid down in Wages Orders. Many workers will be paid more than the nationally agreed minimum entitlement because of special skills, experience, or local negotiation. The average 'basic pay' will therefore tend to be related to the nationally agreed basic wage rates but will generally be higher than those rates.

The difference between percentage movements in total earnings and movements in basic hourly wage rates is known as *earnings drift*. The more commonly heard term *wage drift* is often used as the difference between movements in average hourly earnings, excluding the effects of overtime, and movements in nationally agreed basic hourly wage rates. This term was first used by Hansen and Rehn to describe the 'continuous development of hourly earnings between the discontinuous changes decided upon . . . in collective bargaining' [B 20, page 132]. Much attention has been focused on the concept and movements in wage drift (see in particular J. Marquand's *Wage Drift: Origins, Measurement and Behaviour* [B 28], the Office of Manpower Economics' *Wage Drift* [B 44], and the article in the August 1975 *Gazette* [QRL 24], pages 754–6). The interest in wage drift in the present review arises from the distinction which is made in the literature between earnings, the subject of the present chapter, and wage rates. Until the advent of the NES it was not possible to find a breakdown of total earnings into its various components apart from some limited information in the surveys of earnings by occupation for manual men (Section 5.2.1). Indeed the majority of the tables in the NES as well as all the other official earnings statistics deal with total earnings. Furthermore, these statistics deal almost exclusively with *gross* earnings although figures on *net* earnings (i.e. after deductions for tax and national insurance) are provided from time to time by the Inland Revenue and by income surveys. However, the major series which we shall describe are concerned with *total gross* earnings.

The statistics on earnings are necessarily in a different form from the data on wage rates and salary scales. Those data refer to particular scales of payment agreed nationally and one could imagine the hypothetical example of an individual worker being paid the actual basic rate or salary scale laid down by agreement (although we have emphasized that many workers are paid at other than the basic rate). In contrast the statistics for earnings are necessarily averages or distributions for a whole group of workers. They depend not only on the amount of overtime payments, etc., received, but also on the particular group specified. It is not practicable to list individual earnings, nor would one want such a list, so one uses averages or distributions.

Most of the data we examine will therefore either be sample data, based on sample surveys of individuals or employers, or come from surveys of employers which cover nearly all employees. The earnings of the self-employed are for various institutional reasons extremely difficult to obtain and are always likely to be suspect because of possibilities of under-statement for tax reasons; they have been excluded from the present review.

The coverage of the present earnings statistics is far more extensive than the official wage rates series. The latter are confined to manual workers covered by collective agreements and Wage Councils. Whilst the majority of manual workers are so covered, and are therefore included in the statistics on wage rates, virtually no non-manual workers, now over 40 per cent of all employees according to Elliott [B 9], are covered. As we shall see below, some of the earnings enquiries do cover *all* employees, although there is still more information on manual workers' earnings.

In contrast to the small number of official sources for wage rates (basically only one) and salary scales there is a whole variety of earnings series. Generally-speaking the coverage of the official earnings series is less good for the pre-Second World War period but much better for more recent years, especially since the introduction of the NES in 1968. Because of the wide range of earnings statistics we have decided to concentrate on the three major official series in this chapter and then to devote a separate chapter (Chapter 5) to other official sources and salary surveys. We shall deal first with the monthly index of average earnings (Section 4.2), not because it is the oldest series—it is in fact one of the most recent—but because it provides us with the most up-to-date information on earnings. We shall then discuss the New Earnings Survey (Section 4.3), which is by far the most comprehensive survey. The October earnings survey, which has been carried out continuously since the Second World War, covers manual workers; it is examined in Section 4.4. Information on the historical data is not discussed separately since most of these data will be covered in the section on historical data on earnings (Chapter 7). In Chapter 5 we discuss other rather less important official sources and the very large number of salary surveys.

4.2. Monthly Index of Average Earnings

4.2.1. *Background*

There are two sets of monthly indices of average earnings. The series which is now called the 'older' series was begun in January 1963 by the then Ministry of Labour. The 'new' series, which has a much wider coverage than the 'older' series, was introduced from January 1976 in response to the accepted need for an index covering virtually the whole economy. We shall discuss the 'new' series in Section 4.2.4 but for the moment will confine our attention to the old 'older' series.

The monthly index of average earnings was introduced in 1963 because there was felt to be a need for a rapid, up-to-date indicator of movements in earnings. At that time information on earnings was being compiled only one or twice a year (depending on the series involved) with a publication lag of four months. This meant that there was a most recent information lag of up to ten months. In contrast the wage rates index was being produced each month with a lag of barely a month in publication (Section 2.3.2). But it was widely recognized that the wage rates index was by itself an inadequate indicator of developments on the pay front in the labour market. The wage rates index indicated only what was happening to manual workers' national rates of pay and took no account of developments in overtime and the other components of pay already mentioned, nor of changes determined by local negotiations.

The index was introduced by an article in the April 1963 *Gazette* [QRL 24]. Figures for the first index were based on January 1963, but the base date was soon revised to the average level of 1963 because the abnormally bad weather in the January had caused earnings in some industries to be unusually high and in others correspondingly low. A series of later articles in the *Gazette* explained the revision of the index to the January 1966 base (March 1967) and later to the present January 1970 base (July 1971), and the method of seasonal adjustment of the aggregate series (May 1975). The 'new' series was introduced with an article in the April 1976 *Gazette* (pages 350–2). The 'old' and the 'new' series are now published alongside in Table 129 of each *Gazette*, with industry group indices in, respectively, Table 127 and the Monthly Statistics section of each issue.

4.2.2. *Compilation and coverage*

Information for the monthly index (older series) is mainly collected by a sample survey carried out by the Department each month. About 8,000 large firms in the production industries, transport and communications, and certain miscellaneous services provide returns to the Statistics Division of the Department of Employment. In addition information on agricultural earnings in England and Wales is provided by the Ministry of Agriculture, Fisheries and Food. The sectors not covered include national and local government, distribution, catering, professional and scientific services, and banking, finance, and insurance.

All known firms with over 500 employees are included in the enquiry and below that size a sample of 50 per cent of firms with 100 to 499 employees is taken and 10 per cent of firms with 25 to 99 employees. Firms with less than 25 employees are excluded from the survey. Altogether about 7 million workers are covered in this way—some 60 per cent of all the employees in the industries concerned.

The earnings information for these 7 million workers is obtained by the simplest possible enquiry form (see the specimen form in Appendix C). Employers are asked only five questions each month. These are:

1. The total wages and salaries paid to weekly-paid employees in the last pay week in the month.
2. Holiday pay if paid in advance and included in 1.
3. Total number of weekly-paid employees receiving payment.
4. The total wages and salaries paid to monthly-paid employees in the month.
5. Total number of monthly-paid employees receiving payment.

Employers are specifically requested to include overtime payments, bonuses, commission, etc., and not to make any deductions for tax, national insurance, pension contributions, etc. Fees paid to Directors are excluded and so are employees who are paid other than on a weekly or monthly (or four-weekly) basis, except where large numbers of workers are paid on a fortnightly basis. There is no distinction between men and women, full-time or part-time workers, adults or young people. As can be seen from the specimen form the information is obtained by means of a simple 'shuttle' system, with the same form being sent backwards and forwards each month between the employer and the Department. In contrast to some other official and private forms, this form is very easy to fill in, for most employers will be able to enter the latest month's figures straight from their records.

The earnings of employees who are paid by the month are converted to a weekly basis (multiplying by 12 and dividing by 52). Then total earnings are divided by total employees to obtain the level of average weekly earnings. This is done for most of the individual Minimum List Headings of the industries covered though some have to be grouped. The different sectors are then weighted together in proportion to the total number of employees in each sector. The results are expressed as indices for twenty-three different industrial groupings (SICs XXIII, XXIV, XXV, and XXVII are excluded) and for two aggregate categories, all manufacturing and all industries and services covered. These figures are unadjusted series. But for the two main aggregates seasonally adjusted series are also calculated and shown (see the issues of the *Gazette* [QRL 24] of March 1967, July 1971, May 1975, and February 1977 for a description of the process).

The index of average earnings (older series) is currently based on January 1970 = 100, and uses the 1968 Standard Industrial Classification. The previous series, based on January 1966 = 100, had used the 1958 Standard Industrial Classification (see *Gazette*, March 1967). The original series had also used the 1958 SIC but had a base of January 1963 = 100 and later 1963 = 100. In deriving a long, monthly series dating back to the first figures in 1963 the usual problems of linking different series exist. Because the series is currently weighted the problems of linkage are, however, not as large as in a base weighted series. The Department published linked series for the whole of the period from January 1963 to mid 1971 for the two main series in a *Gazette* article in July 1971 (pages 613–15). Both the unadjusted and seasonally adjusted series are shown in that article, all on a base of January 1970 = 100. The percentage increases in the seasonally adjusted index compared with the corresponding month in the previous year are also tabulated and there is some discussion of the problems of seasonally adjusting the earnings series. A later set of figures for the period 1963–74 including new seasonal adjustments was published in the article in the May 1975 *Gazette*. Since the beginning of 1977 a long series of the monthly data has also been published each month in Table 129 of the *Gazette*.

The index becomes available in provisional form about six to seven weeks after the month to which it relates. But it is subject to revision in the following month when information on late returns and for agriculture is taken into account. The revisions are only slight, being generally something like 0.1–0.2 per cent of the total index level.

Irregular movements in pay arise due to variations in overtime pay, bonus payments, backdated pay, and sickness. The compilers of the index therefore warn that

> '. . . some fluctuations in the index from month to month are therefore to be expected, even after adjustment for normal seasonal variations. Consequently too much weight should not be given to the precise value of the index in a particular month, and it is generally advisable to have regard to a run of figures for a few months.' (*Gazette* [QRL 24], July 1971, page 614.)

The last caveat should perhaps be restated and borne in mind for all the statistical series which we examine in this review.

When the results of the monthly average earnings index for manufacturing are compared with the results of the far more detailed NES and October earnings surveys (see Sections 4.3 and 4.4), it is found that the year-to-year changes in earnings are very nearly the same in both cases. In the July 1971 *Gazette* article this comparison is made and there is also an attempt to allow for the fact of changing composition in the work-force on the earnings figures. Some of the movement in the monthly index of average earnings is due not to movements in individuals' earnings but to changes in the relative proportions of men and women, manual and non-manual, or full-time and part-time employees. These particular movements arise because the monthly index, in contrast to the wage rates index, effectively uses current weights. An exercise conducted on the October earnings enquiry using fixed weights for the industry groups (to abstract from changing composition) has shown that

> '. . . though the effect of changing composition is not negligible, it is generally less than the effect of variations in earnings in particular months.' (*Gazette* [QRL 24], July 1971, page 614.)

The crucial difference between the current weighted earnings series and the base weighted wage rates series is often forgotten by the users of these statistics. Furthermore, since the earnings series covers all workers whilst the wage rates index covers only manual workers, any comparison between the two must be made with care. However, wage drift is often measured as the difference between the movements in these two series. Such a calculation is incorrect but is often justified as an *ad hoc* procedure for the short term. The monthly index refers to Great Britain only, with the exception of agriculture which refers to England and Wales only. The coverage of the index has remained the same but for two small changes in the earlier years. From August 1963, London Transport was included in the enquiry, and from October 1966, British Road Services. The extension of the inquiry to other industries and services in 1976 is discussed separately in Section 4.2.4 on the 'new' series.

4.2.3. *Availability*

The latest figures for the monthly index of average earnings are published in each month's *Gazette* [QRL 24]. Full details, including separate indices for the twenty-three main industry groups and the unadjusted and seasonally adjusted figures for manufacturing and all industries, are given for several previous years in Table 127. The all industries figures are released in a departmental Press Notice about a week or two before the publication of the *Gazette*, and are usually recorded and commented upon in the main daily newspapers. In addition, a run of monthly figures for the old index over ten years and for the new index (see Section 4.2.4) since it started in 1976, plus annual percentage increases for both services, has been given in Table 129 of the *Gazette* since February 1977.

The average-earnings figures are also reproduced in other official sources. The *Monthly Digest of Statistics* [QRL 52] gives the index in the same detail as the *Gazette* but for only up to two and a half years. *Economic Trends* [QRL 27] gives quarterly and annual averages of the seasonally adjusted index for all industries and services and manufacturing industries (older series) for the latest six years, and the *Economic Trends Annual Supplement* [QRL 28] provides quarterly averages since the index started in 1963. The *British Labour Statistics Yearbook* [QRL 19] gives annual indices for all the industrial groups for about four years and the *Annual Abstract of Statistics* [QRL 13] gives the same coverage as the *Gazette* for ten years. Lastly, the *British Labour Statistics; Historical Abstract* [QRL 18] gives a complete series for all the industry groups for the period 1963–68 on the 1966 base (Table 56). Users of the seasonally adjusted data are advised to try to obtain the latest available series since from time to time the seasonally adjusted series are revised as additional years are taken into account in the adjustment procedure. This warning applies more generally to all seasonally adjusted data. Such revisions, which average less than half a per cent, can be as much as 2 per cent up or down in the seasonally adjusted average earnings series; they are rarely more than 0.2 per cent in the unadjusted series.

4.2.4. *The 'new' series (1976)*

The restricted coverage of the 'older' series increasingly became a problem since the excluded sectors (which included public administration, distribution, catering, professional and scientific services, and banking, insurance, and finance) happened to be rather important areas of employment growth in the economy.

There was a realization that information covering the whole economy was needed. The Department therefore extended the older monthly index to the rest of the economy as from the beginning of 1976. The introduction of this new index is described in an article in the April 1976 *Gazette*. In addition to the previous coverage, returns are now also obtained from education authorities, government departments, local authorities, the National Health Service, the Post Office, the larger banks, building societies, finance houses and insurance companies, the wholesale and retail distributive trades, and the catering and entertainment industries.

The new index, for which there are returns covering about 10,500 firms and organizations and some 12 million workers, is representative of the whole economy.

The exact differences in coverage between the older and new series are explained in Table 3, which is now published every month in the *Gazette*.

With a few minor exceptions the 'new' series covers the whole economy. Fishing and sea transport (in SIC Orders I and XXII) are excluded because of the difficulties in covering these areas satisfactorily in a short-term enquiry. In professional and scientific services (SIC Order XXV), information is obtained only from local educational services and the National Health Service. The universities, private educational establishments, and accountancy, legal, research, and various other services are not covered. Lastly, in the financial sector (SIC Order XXIV), information is collected from insurance companies, banks, building societies, and finance houses only. In all these cases the number of employees not covered is relatively small. The largest omission in the enquiry is those firms with less than twenty-five employees. In a short-term enquiry it is

TABLE 3. *Coverage of the 'new' monthly index of average earnings*

SIC Order	Type*	Industry
I to XXVII	B	Whole economy
I	C	Agriculture and forestry
II	A	Mining and quarrying
III to XIX	C	All manufacturing industries
III	A	Food, drink, and tobacco
IV	A	Coal and petroleum products
V	A	Chemicals and allied industries
VI	A	Metal manufacture
VII	C	Mechanical engineering
VIII	A	Instrument engineering
IX	A	Electrical engineering
X	C	Shipbuilding and marine engineering
XI	A	Vehicles
XII	A	Metal goods not elsewhere specified
XIII	A	Textiles
XIV	A	Leather, leather goods, and fur
XV	A	Clothing and footwear
XVI	A	Bricks, pottery, glass, cement, etc.
XVII	A	Timber, furniture, etc.
XVIII	C	Paper, printing, and publishing
XIX	A	Other manufacturing industries
XX	C	Construction
XXI	A	Gas, electricity, and water
XXII	C	Transport and communication
XXIII	B	Distributive trades
XXIV	B	Insurance, banking, and finance
XXV	B	Professional and scientific services
XXVI	C	Miscellaneous services
XXVII	B	Public administration

*The types of series are categorized as follows:
Type A. Those for which indices were available before January 1976.
Type B. Those for which indices were not available before January 1976.
Type C. Those for which indices were available before January 1976, but with narrower coverage than those now available.

not practicable to try to attempt to cover these, and in any case it probably makes virtually no difference when measuring changes in average earnings.

Both indices are now being produced each month. The new index is reported in the Monthly Statistics section of the *Gazette* [QRL 24] from April 1976. As from the February 1977 *Gazette* figures for the 'new' series whole economy index began to appear alongside those for the 'older' series, all industries and services and all manufacturing in a new Table 129, and in the Press Notice issued when the figures are released. In the first year of the 'new' series (January 1976 to January 1977) the 'new' all industries index rose by 10.9 per cent compared with the rise of 12.0 per cent in the old index over the same period. This shows the close similarity of the two series. For long runs of historical figures one will still have to use the 'older' series, but for recent movements in earnings the more comprehensive 'new' series probably gives a better indication of yearly increases in earnings in the economy as a whole. However, the new series cannot yet be seasonally adjusted since several years of data are needed to obtain estimates of normal seasonal movements. It is therefore sensible that the 'new' and 'older' series will both continue to be published for the indefinite future.

As well as being published in the Monthly Statistics section and Table 129 of the *Gazette* [QRL 24] the 'new' series is given in many of the other sources where the 'older' series is presently available (see Section 4.2.3). The detailed figures on different industries are not given in the *Gazette* but appear in the *Monthly Digest of Statistics* [QRL 52].

4.3. New Earnings Survey [QRL 55]

4.3.1. *Introduction*

The *New Earnings Survey* [QRL 55] was first introduced in Great Britain in 1968 to provide a more detailed source of information on earnings than the existing sources. For many groups of non-manual workers, particularly in the service industries, this new survey provides the only information on their earnings. The survey is based on a 1 per cent random sample of employees and provides a very detailed examination of levels, distributions, and the make-up of earnings of employees by occupation, industry, agreement, region, and various personal characteristics. The sampling rate, which is given with the NES results, is generally about 1 in 130 employees in employment. The survey is confined to Great Britain, with Northern Ireland data being collected separately.

The first NES carried out by the Department of Employment related to September 1968. This was in some senses a trial run for a new survey on earnings, although a small-scale pilot survey had already been conducted. The earnings and other particulars of about 84,000 employees, selected by a random sample of half a per cent of employees in employment, were collected in this first survey. Following this first NES survey in 1968 an expert group, including representatives of the CBI and the TUC, was appointed by the Department of Employment and Productivity to make recommendations on the future of the NES and of the other regular official earnings surveys. Their report is reproduced as Appendix V of the 1968 *New Earnings Survey* [QRL 55], pages 190–2. The expert group recommended that the survey should be held in April each year, starting in April 1970, and that the sample size should be doubled. As part of the 'package' for continuing the NES in its revised form the previous April part of the biannual manual workers' earnings enquiry (Section 4.4) was discontinued, apart from a few minor industries (Section 5.2.2), and the October salary survey into the earnings of administrative, technical, and clerical employees was also stopped (Section 5.3.2), although it was later reinstated for the EEC (Section 5.3.4).

The changes in the NES between 1968 and 1970 were quite substantial (although the largest changes came with the streamlining of the survey in 1971). The survey questionnaire used in 1968 was a fairly long six-page form. The questionnaire was then reduced in length and the questions were modified in the light of the comments of the expert group and following consultations with other interested parties. These developments in the survey are described in Section 4.3.4.

The results of the 1968 survey were first published in instalments in the *Gazette* [QRL 24] between May and October 1969. The full results were then published in a single volume, *New Earnings Survey 1968* [QRL 55], in 1970. This was the pattern of publication up to 1973. Since 1974, however, the key results have been published within six months in the October *Gazette* and the full results have been published in a six-part publication; the six separate parts become available at monthly intervals from October. The publication lag is now much less than the original nine to eighteen months of the 1968 survey. The whole series of separate parts is completed in less than a year from the survey date and, in addition, a set of streamlined analyses by industry, occupation, and agreement, and a selection of general results are published in the *Gazette* in October.

The first survey relating to September 1968 was followed by a second relating to April 1970 and there have subsequently been New Earnings Surveys for every April since then. The changes in the format of the NES since 1968 are discussed in Section 4.3.4, but as the format is now fairly settled we firstly examine that of the more recent surveys.

4.3.2. *Compilation*

The *New Earnings Survey* [QRL 55] is a 1 per cent sample survey of the earnings of employees in April each year carried out by the Department of Employment. Unlike the monthly index of average earnings (Section 4.2) the survey covers employees in all sizes of business, although along with most of the other earnings surveys, the self-employed are excluded. The survey is carried out under the Statistics of Trade Act, 1947, with the type of form which is reproduced in Appendix D. Employers are obliged to return the forms for all employees for whom information is requested. For large companies or organizations this may require the filling in of quite a lot of forms, but the information requested is of the sort that is usually readily available, although some employers have difficulties. However, many small firms may not be involved at all and only about 1,200 pay offices have to fill in more than twenty forms.

The survey is based on a random 1 per cent sample of employees. All those with national insurance numbers ending with one specified pair of digits are included in the sample, and this pair of digits is retained for a period of years so that 'matched' samples are available. Of those employees who are covered in two successive years, in practice about two-thirds are in the matched sample. It is not an easy procedure to trace employees with the given national insurance numbers. It was originally done through national insurance cards but since they were abolished in 1975 new procedures have had to be adopted.

Since 1975 the employees in the sample have been traced through the records of the Pay-As-You-Earn (PAYE) schemes. The Inland Revenue, under the authorization of Section 58 of the Finance Act 1969, notifies the Department of Employment of the names and addresses of the employers of the relevant employees. This information is elicited from the PAYE records in February/March and the forms are sent out as soon as possible thereafter. Unfortunately in some respects the coverage is now less comprehensive than before 1975 because not all employees are covered by PAYE schemes and the Inland Revenue tax offices do not always hold records in February/March showing the current employer for employees who changed jobs in the previous two or three months. The survey excludes most of those whose weekly or monthly earnings are below the deduction card limits for tax purposes. These are mostly young persons and part-time workers, in particular women, since few full-time adult workers are not in PAYE schemes. On the other hand, if someone is a member of more than one PAYE scheme because of holding more than one job then two different records of earnings by that person are recorded although the two are part of one income (see the discussion of definitions in Section 1.1). In this respect the sample is slightly larger since subsidiary employments were previously excluded. The sample is therefore somewhat different from earlier years. In particular the part-time employees covered in the sample are no longer representative of part-time workers generally.

Once the names and addresses of the relevant employers have been obtained from the Inland Revenue, the forms (like that in Appendix D) are sent out, one for each employee covered. The information requested concerns the earnings of the individual employee during the particular pay period which includes the *survey reference date* (4 April in 1979), even if that employee's earnings have been affected by absence during that period.

The information provided by employers is treated as strictly confidential. The name of the individual employee is only given on a perforated slip at the top of the questionnaire which the employer is asked to detach before returning the form. The original forms are destroyed after an interval and the magnetic tapes which are retained do not identify either the name or address of either the employer or the employee. The information obtained covers a variety of questions concerned with

1. Total earnings.
2. Overtime earnings and hours.
3. Payment by results, etc., shift premium payments, etc.
4. Normal basic hours.
5. Whether within scope of Wages Board or Wages Council.
6. Whether affected by one of a list of collective agreements, directly or indirectly, and, if so, which one.
7. Sex and year of birth.
8. Location of work-place.
9. Occupation.

The exact wording of all the 1978 questions is shown in the specimen form (Appendix D). These questions are elaborated on in the Description of the Survey in Part A, Report and Key results (pages A38–A44) of the *New Earnings Survey 1978* [QRL 55].

The published results give cross-tabulations of the various answers for different groups of workers classified by sex, age, occupation, industry, region, and agreement. All sorts of other results are theoretically derivable. Information in a more detailed form can be obtained from the Department if it has already been produced internally. Special analyses in addition to those carried out by the Department are generally not available although such analyses have in special circumstances sometimes been made (see, for instance, the work by Mulvey [B 29] analysing the 1973 results by agreement). However, in such cases the user is charged and if necessary must provide the computer programme. It is also possible for companies to obtain, by prior arrangement, an analysis of the data that they have provided for the NES. Problems can sometimes arise where delayed settlements have had a retrospective effect on earnings. An important example of this occurred in 1975. The non-industrial Civil Service received a large pay rise (it entailed a substantial catching-up element) in May 1975 which was backdated to 1 January 1975. Because the settlement was agreed after the survey returns for the April 1975 NES had been completed, the pay rise was not reflected in the 1975 NES results. Since this pay rise happened to be an extremely large one the omission was noted by various commentators (see, for instance, Dean's 'Why public sector pay is still a battlefield' [B 5]). This particular omission was specifically noted in the 1976 NES (see pages A48–A49) but the problem is that in most cases such backdating goes unnoticed. It might therefore be sensible to ask a subsidiary question about the possibility of any future settlement being backdated to the survey reference period.

Another problem that often arises but is also difficult to deal with is the shift in settlement dates around the time of the April survey. If a settlement has been brought forward from after April to before it, or vice-versa, the movement in earnings for that group may seem extreme compared with other groups. The NES now footnotes those figures which are known to have been affected by a delayed settlement, though they cannot hope to be aware of all such cases. This problem is of course not unique to the NES but just underlines the fact that one must be very careful to weigh up all the circumstances when using such data.

4.3.3. *Presentation of the results*

The results of the 1977 NES were presented in the following six parts:

Part A. Report and key results.
Part B. Analyses by agreement.
Part C. Analyses by industry.
Part D. Analyses by occupation.
Part E. Analyses by region and age group.
Part F. Hours.
            Earnings by type of incentive payment.
            Earnings of part-time workers.

Parts A to E are now in a standard form and do not change from year to year. The analyses in Part F vary slightly as special questions come and go.

Part A gives an introduction to the survey of the particular year, shows the response rate, and outlines the key results. It is therefore the most useful part for someone who does not want to look through the vast number of tabulations in the five other parts of the NES although the best summary is provided in the regular article in the October *Gazette*. In 1976 170,000 satisfactorily completed returns were received in time for processing. Of these, 145,000 represented full-time employees in employment in Great Britain in April 1976. The coverage of full-time men (1 in 120) was slightly greater than that of full-time women (1 in 130). A further 16,000 questionnaires were returned uncompleted for various reasons and a further 9,000 were not returned in time for processing. The 'matched' sample covered 115,000 employees for whom 1975 returns had also been received, i.e. two-thirds of the total sample. A fuller categorization of the sample is given in Table 21 of Part A and also in tables in the other parts.

The earnings figures recorded are average gross weekly earnings for different groups of workers. Most of the results take those employees whose pay was not affected by absence but (lower) results are also given for groups including those so affected. Average gross hourly earnings are also given and both sets of results are broken down to give comprehensive results for the distribution of earnings. The average make-up of pay, by the fourfold subdivision already mentioned, is calculated for a variety of groups. Separate tables are generally given for full-time manual men, non-manual men, manual women, and non-manual women. The distribution of normal basic hours is also recorded for different workers according to whether they are male or female, part-time or full-time, manual or non-manual, and adult or young person.

At the back of Part A there is a full description of the survey. There are also appendices giving

1. The survey questionnaire.
2. Grouped lists of occupations used in the survey.
3. List of major collective agreements and Wage Boards and Councils used in the survey.
4. List of regions and sub-regions.
5. Glossary of terms and definitions.

Parts B, C, D, and E give the same sort of results concerning the distribution and make-up of pay as Part A, but give far more detail for different agreements, industries, occupations and regions, and age groups. Individual collective agreements are cited in Part B, providing a useful contrast to the official wage rates data which are compiled using much the same classification. The figures on the sample size for each agreement give a rough idea of the numbers affected by these agreements. It should be noted that employees affected both directly and indirectly are identified.

Part C gives results by industry, going down to MLH level where the sample size is large enough. Results are generally given only for those industries represented by at least one hundred persons in the sample.

This particular test for inclusion is applied to most of the tabulations. The results published for women workers are therefore not as extensive as those for men because of the smaller numbers involved. However, many of the tables throughout the NES are foot-noted to the effect that the corresponding results for those groups excluded on the grounds of sample size are available on request. Averages are generally given only if the percentage standard error is not more than 2.0 per cent, but distribution and quantities are given for a wider range of industries.

Part D analyses the results by particular occupations. The classification system used is based on the Department of Employment List of Key Occupations for Statistical

Purposes (KOS) (see September 1972 *Gazette* [QRL 24] pages 799–801). The list is reproduced in Appendix 2 of Part A. This is a different classification to that used prior to 1973 (see Section 4.3.4). There were also minor differences between the 1976 and 1975 NES. The recalculated and reclassified results for civil servants (pages A48–A49) have already been mentioned (in Section 4.3.2). Otherwise the group 'general administrators—local government' was previously described as 'local government officers not identified elsewhere', these results being published together with 'town clerks and other clerks to local authorities.'

Part E gives the regional analyses and a breakdown by age group. The regional results are given not only by Standard Region but also by Metropolitan County, County, or Greater London Borough. The classification is that arising from the reorganization of local government in 1974/5 and is given in Appendix 4 of Part A. There are also tables which include earnings figures by industrial and occupational groups for each Standard Region (Tables 118–23). The analysis by age group gives the average, the distribution, and the make-up of pay with a cross-classification by occupational group. Nine age groups are listed. There are also some figures in Part E on the classification of the sample by numbers and length of service for each group. This particular information, though only a restricted sample, provides useful information to back up the Census of Population and Census of Employment figures.

Part F covers hours, earnings by length of service, earnings of part-time workers, and some joint distributions of hours and earnings and overtime hours and normal hours. Much of the information of this type cannot be found elsewhere. Indeed, the majority of the NES data are unique. Whilst attention has tended to focus on the average earnings and distribution figures, which are the core of the NES, much of the other information on numbers, hours, age, occupation, and so on, is equally valuable though so far largely unused.

An important feature of the NES results is the availability of matched samples. These arise because the same final two digits of the national insurance numbers are used each year for selecting the sample. The size of the matched sample is usually about two-thirds of the size of the full sample because the response rate is not 100 per cent and because demographic movements and changes in employee status reduce the size of the matched sample every year. One should note, however, that while the complete sample is a random sample of the whole population of employees who are working at a given date, and the matched sample is a random sample of those who worked in two successive Aprils, nevertheless these two populations are different. Consequently the complete and the matched samples are measuring different things. For example, the matched sample shows the effects of annual salary increments on the earnings of individuals. These are not apparent from the complete samples because of the offsetting effects of retirements and recruitments. The matched sample will exclude the person who is 21 (and has therefore just qualified as adult) and the person who has just retired. This will tend to inflate the average earnings that are recorded. On the other hand, the use of the matched sample does indicate exactly what has happened to the earnings of a fixed group of people during the year in question. The matched sample is a new idea in published government statistics and provides a unique set of data. Results for matched samples have been available each year since 1971 in the NES results, but always for successive years rather than a run of years. However, two studies in the April 1973 and January 1977 issues of the *Gazette* [QRL 24] have used runs of figures over the years 1970–2 and 1970–4 respectively. These studies show how the earnings of particular individuals have changed over a number of years. Unfortunately an extension of the analysis to 1975 is not possible because of the discontinuity in the sample introduced by the switch from the national insurance card basis to PAYE records. However, analyses of the data from 1975 onwards will be possible.

4.3.4. *Developments in the NES since 1968*

We have already mentioned (in Section 4.3.1) that the coverage and form of publication of the NES has changed somewhat since the original survey in September 1968. Although the format has now become fairly fixed (and is much as described in Section 4.3.2), it is worth noting the main developments in the survey, especially as some of the interesting information that is provided by the NES is collected only intermittently. The general aim, according to the Department, is

'. . . to keep most of the survey questions unchanged from year to year, so that directly comparable results are obtained. However, questions are not retained when the information is no longer regarded as essential. On some topics information is not necessary every year, and so they can be covered adequately by questions at intervals of several years.' (*New Earnings Survey 1976* [QRL 55], Part A, page A37.)

Continuity in the NES from year to year has certainly been the situation in recent years, for the NES since 1974, when the results started to be published in its six-part booklet form, has changed very little, with the kind of results given and the table numbers used being almost identical.

The actual survey questionnaire used in each survey is shown in an appendix to each of the annual volumes up to 1973 and in Part A since 1974. We have already referred to the 1968 form, which ran to six pages and is reproduced in Appendix E, and also to the 1978 form, only two pages long, shown in Appendix D. An examination of successive questionnaires indicates how the information requested has changed each year, but here we shall concentrate only on the changes in the published results and in the major questions used. Further information on changes from year to year is available in the introductory sections of each NES (as a special chapter in the 1970, 1971, and 1972 NES).

4.3.4.1. *Changes in the published results*

The most important changes between the first two NES of 1968 and 1970 were in the sample size and in the way the results were tabulated. The first NES, of 1968, was very much an experimental run, with a sample size only half that of the later surveys. The results were published to give as much information as possible on distributions of earnings. Although the information on distribution of earnings was retained for all subsequent NES, this strong emphasis on distribution in the 1968 NES was relaxed. It is extremely difficult to find information on *average* earnings in that first survey; one can only find such figures by implication, and one is forced to calculate the figures from the other data. The reason why average earnings figures were not published in 1968, given in Appendix IV of the *New Earnings Survey 1968* [QRL 55], is that such figures were difficult to reconcile with the existing October enquiry (Section 4.4).

The full description of changes between the first two NES is provided in Chapter 4 of the *New Earnings Survey 1970* [QRL 55] pages 18–21. Apart from the change in sample size most of the changes were of a minor nature. In the 1968 survey, for instance, the employer was asked whether the employee normally received tips and gratuities, but in the 1970 survey (and subsequently) this question was dropped. There were other small changes of this sort plus several changes in classification; the 1968 SIC replaced that of 1958, sixteen main occupational groups replaced the previous ten, although within the groups there was a high correspondence with the previous occupations. Policemen, firemen, and shop assistants, who were classified as manual in 1968, were treated as non-manual in 1970. The effect of all these changes is that many of the 1968 survey analyses were not obtained in 1970 and many of the 1970 survey analyses were new ones. As a consequence of these changes the results of the 1968 and 1970 surveys are not comparable in all respects. A summary of the 1970 tables which correspond to the 1968 NES is given in Appendix IV of the *New Earnings Survey 1970*, page 264, where the main differences in the tables are also listed.

The 1970 NES may be regarded as the first full survey. The correspondence between the 1970 survey and later volumes is thus much closer than that between the 1968 and 1970 surveys. However, the 1971 survey used a much shortened and simplified questionnaire in order to reduce the burden of form-filling. The changes between the 1970 and 1971 surveys are fully described in Chapter 4, *New Earnings Survey 1971* [QRL 55] pages 25–7. The correspondence between tables in the 1970 and 1971 NES is also given in Appendix IV, page 242, and in addition underneath the title of each table in the 1971 NES there is a reference to the corresponding table in the 1970 volume. This practice was continued in the 1972, 1973, and 1974 surveys. However, as from 1975 the table numbering has remained the same except for one or two minor changes which are pointed out in the same way (with a reference under the table title).

The 1972 NES was much like the 1971 survey apart from the publication of some additional information on the earnings and hours of part-time women. There was also an annex on low pay and changes in earnings which had originally been published in the April 1973 *Gazette* [QRL 24]. Chapter 3 of the *New Earnings Survey 1972*, page 22, contains a full description of changes between the 1971 and 1972 NES. The Appendix IV, page 278, gives a comparison of the table numbers in the 1970, 1971, and 1972 NES.

As from the 1973 NES, the regular separate chapter explaining the differences between that and previous surveys was discontinued, mainly because these differences from year to year had by now become slight as the format of the NES had became more fixed. However, the changes in the latest survey are always mentioned in the introduction or description of the survey; see, for instance, the introduction to the *New Earnings Survey 1973*, page ii. The main changes in the 1973 survey were the new occupational classification (mentioned in the next section) and the calculation of hourly earnings which now excluded those people affected by absence. Appendix IV of the 1973 NES gave the usual comparison of table numbers between the 1973 and 1972 surveys.

The 1974 NES volume had a changed format, now being produced in six parts, but otherwise remained much the same as the previous survey. The introduction in Part A of the *New Earnings Survey 1974* [QRL 55] page A36, explained the differences in the questionnaire. These were the dropping of the 1973 question on the type of collective agreement (if any) which affected the employee concerned, the introduction of a question on annual entitlements to paid holiday, and a new sub-regional classification due to the reorganization of local government. This reorganization led to an under-representation of employees in local authorities in England and Wales and in the separately reorganized National Health Service (see NES 1974, page A41). The Appendix giving the comparison of table numbers with the previous NES was dropped. It was now thought sufficient to have the relevant reference to the corresponding table of the previous NES under the table title (as had happened since the 1971 NES).

The 1975 NES, however, was so like the 1974 NES in table numbering that even this practice was dropped apart from the few tables in Parts E and F where changes had been made. The questions on training and holidays in the 1974 NES were now dropped but an extra question on length of service with the present company was inserted. There were also some extra questions in this survey for the retail, wholesale distribution, banking, and insurance sectors to conform with EEC requirements. These extra questions were described in Chapter 1 of Part A (pages A43–44) of the *New Earnings Survey 1975* [QRL 55] and the results were given in Part F, pages F61–3, and were also published by the Statistical Office of the European Communities. Due to the change to a PAYE basis for tracing the sample (see Section 4.3.2) the coverage of part-timers was much reduced as from 1975.

The 1976 NES dropped the special section of EEC questions, which were no longer required, but all the other questions from the 1975 survey were retained and no new ones were added. The table numbering was for the first time exactly the same as in the previous survey. Indeed, since the introduction of the six-part volume in 1974, the ordering of the results has remained very much the same and it is therefore much easier to trace particular results for different years back through successive volumes. Because of the confusion caused by the backdating of some awards in 1975, particularly concerning civil servants (see Section 4.3.2), special emphasis was put on the possibility of of this arising in 1976 (see *New Earnings Survey 1976*, pages A48–9). Some results from 1975 were also recalculated to take account of occupational misclassification (*op. cit.*, Table 2, Part A).

The 1977 NES again remained much the same as that of the previous year. The length of service question was dropped and a new question on types of incentive payments was used. The employer was asked to record if the employee in question had received incentive payments and, if so, whether such payments were dependent on the perfor-mance of the individual, a group of employees, or the whole company or establishment. He was then asked how performance was measured; whether by piece-work, allowed times, the value of work done, sales, value added, profit, or 'other' means.

The 1978 NES dropped the question on the type of incentive payments and asked instead about the type of collective agreement, if any, which affected the employee in question. There was also, for the first time, a breakdown of the NES results for the public and private sectors (see *New Earnings Survey 1978*, page A6). These sectoral results, with the public sector broken down into central government, local government, and public corporations, show average gross weekly earnings, the percentage increase between 1977 and 1978 for the complete samples, and the dispersion of gross weekly earnings around the median (lowest and highest deciles, and lower and upper quartiles). The publication of these figures, which update figures for the 1970–7 period contained in the December 1977 *Gazette*, is very welcome. Previous analyses of public and private sector pay, such as Dean's analysis of manual workers' earnings over the period 1950–75 [QRL 3], had had to rely on less specific data. The new NES data in this area is excellent because it is able to give a male/female and manual/non-manual breakdown, although it only goes back to 1970. For an analysis over a longer period of time one must go back to Dean [QRL 3] or to Elliott's article on public sector wage movements [B 11]. For the future, however, figures on public and private sector pay will be published each year in the *New Earnings Survey*.

The 1979 NES re-introduced the length of service question and introduced some other minor changes to try to meet the requirements of the EEC structure of earnings survey.

The pattern of New Earnings Surveys tables since 1974 has been fairly standard and the questions have remained largely unchanged since 1972. The large majority of questions are retained each year and the results of these appear in the same tables from year to year. A special question (sometimes two) appears each year, but is then dropped from the survey in the succeeding year, being replaced by another special question. An example of these is the question on holiday entitlements in 1974. But despite the change with this special question almost all the tables retain their numbering from year to year so that it is now very easy to trace a continuous series. This does not mean that changes cannot be made to the NES, but its format is clearly fairly settled and all the major questions are now likely to stay.

4.3.4.2. *Major changes in the questions asked or classifications used*

Since the NES started in 1968 there have been three major changes in classification:

1. The sub-regional classification was changed in 1974 following the reorganization of local government in England and Wales and the prospective change in Scottish local government in 1975. Previously standard sub-divisions of regions had been used. In 1974 they were replaced by the newly formed counties, metropolitan boroughs, and boroughs as listed in Appendix 4 of the 1974 NES, page A56, and as described in the same volume, page E2. The regions themselves were not changed from the 1973 classification but the sub-regions were almost entirely redefined.

2. The occupational classification was changed in 1973 to the newly introduced List of Key Occupations for Statistical Purposes (KOS). This classification is a much expanded version of the previous list with about 400 occupations specified compared with about 200 before. The full list is given as Appendix II of the *New Earnings Survey 1973* [QRL 55] pages 285–7, and is also reproduced as an appendix to Part A of subsequent volumes. The pre-1973 classification is shown as Appendix II of the *New Earnings Survey 1972*, pages 275–6. Because of the major change in the number of occupations listed it is not possible, except in a limited number of cases, to make comparisons between the figures before and after 1973.

3. The industrial classification was changed in the 1970 NES to the 1968 SIC from the 1958 SIC which had been used in the 1968 NES.

Apart from these changes in classification, the main changes in the questions have been as follows.

The *make-up of pay* question was included up to 1970, was absent in 1971 and 1972 (although overtime pay was still recorded), and then was reintroduced in 1973 with a more aggregated classification. The original categories of pay delineated in the 1968 and 1970 NES were: basic pay, overtime pay, shift, and other premium payments, PBR, bonus, commission, and other pay. In 1971 and 1972 only overtime pay was separately categorized. When the make-up of pay question was reintroduced in 1973 a fourfold classification was used; overtime pay and shift and other premium payments remained as two separate categories, but other pay was put with basic pay to give 'all other pay', and PBR, bonus, and commission were combined together as PBR, etc., payments.

Information on the *annual entitlement to paid holiday* was obtained in 1968, 1970, and 1974. In the earlier period the answer was given in working days and additional holiday entitlements due to length of service were separately specified in 1970. In the 1974 survey the answer was given in terms of working weeks and days and no further details were requested.

The *length of service* question was part of the 1968 survey. A question on whether employment had lasted twelve months was substituted for the next five surveys. The length of service question was included again in 1975 and 1976 and then dropped completely in 1977.

The question on *whether the employee is affected by a collective agreement* specified in a list of major agreements has always been asked. However, in 1968, 1970, 1973, and 1978 more detailed information was requested, the employer being asked to indicate the *type of collective agreement* affecting the pay of the employee under various headings. In 1973 and 1978 these headings were:

1. National agreement and supplementary company/district/local agreement.
2. National agreement only.
3. Company/district/local agreement only.
4. No collective agreement.

A list of the major national agreements has always been provided for the employer so that he can specify the actual agreement, if any, which affects a particular employee. This list, which was substantially revised in 1977, is reproduced as an Appendix to each survey (e.g. Appendix 3 of the *New Earnings Survey 1977* [QRL 55], pages A55–6). The categorization of workers according to this list is the basis of Part B of the NES on Analyses by Agreement.

4.4. October Earnings Survey

4.4.1. *Origins*

Information on the earnings and hours of *manual* workers has been obtained by the Department of Employment from a sample of employers at various times since 1886. Up to the Second World War these enquiries were conducted fairly irregularly in 1886, 1906, 1924, 1928, 1931, 1935, and 1938. A greater degree of regularity was then introduced with enquiries in July 1940 and July 1941 and then in each January and July from 1942 to January 1946. From October 1946 these six-monthly enquiries were switched from January and July to April and October. Up to 1969 these enquiries continued to be held twice a year. Then, in 1970, the *New Earnings Survey* [QRL 55] (Section 4.3) replaced the previous April enquiry so that the manual workers' enquiry is now held only once a year in October. For this reason we have called it here the *October Earnings Survey* (OES), although this is not the official name for it, nor is the title strictly correct before 1970. A few industries are still covered in April each year by a vestige of the former April enquiry but these are very limited in number and are not of major importance (see Section 5.2.2).

The results of the 1886 and 1906 enquiries were published as special reports. The next four enquiries (1924, 1928, 1931, and 1935) were published in separate instalments in the *Gazette* [QRL 24] in several successive issues starting in June 1926, October 1929, January 1933, and February 1937. The results of the earnings enquiries for 1938 and the war years were published together in the August 1944 and February 1945 *Gazettes*. Since 1946 the results of the enquiries have been regularly published in the *Gazette* about four months after the date of the enquiry. At the present time the October enquiry results are published in a special article in the *Gazette* in the following February (although in 1977, due to an industrial dispute, the results were not published until March). The results of this October enquiry cannot be compared directly with the results for manual workers of the April NES, although movements in the two series over a period of time tend to be very close (see the discussion in Appendix IV of the *New Earnings Survey 1968*, pages 188–9).

The development of the manual workers' enquiry since 1886 is described in the chapter by Ainsworth in Kendall's *Sources and Nature of Statistics of the United Kingdom* [B 23], so we shall only outline the major changes here. The original enquiries of 1886 and 1906 used information on the earnings and hours of individuals and were therefore able to give details for the distribution of earnings as well as averages for separate occupations. Later enquiries, with a few exceptions, asked employers only for total numbers employed, total wages paid, and total hours worked for men, women, boys, and girls. Weekly and hourly averages for each industry were therefore available. The exceptions were 1938 and 1960 when individual particulars were obtained (so that it was possible to calculate distributions), 1960, when firms were asked to give information on distributions, and 1940 to January 1943, when hours worked were not requested.

Since 1924 the coverage has included all manufacturing industries and a few services originally associated with manufacturing (see Section 4.4.2). However, additional information has usually been obtained from various public sector bodies on earnings in agriculture, coal-mining, the railways, and the docks, though the latter is now included in the survey (see Section 5.2.3). Figures for these industries are also published in the *Gazette*, either in the article describing the results of the latest OES, or separately.

Separate figures by industry have been published since 1924 (the two earlier enquiries giving an occupational breakdown). The classification has changed somewhat during the period so that comparison of inter-war and post-war industrial figures is not easy. In particular the introduction of the new SIC in 1948 gave a more detailed industrial classification. The SIC changes in 1958 and 1968 were of much smaller importance.

Although the industrial coverage has changed very little since 1924, the number of firms covered has fluctuated. Thus the 1938 enquiry covered all employers with more than ten workers and a fifth of all others. Over 70 per cent of the total employees in the industries concerned were covered by the replies. The list of firms is continuously updated. Altogether returns are now sent to nearly 40,000 establishments with over 5 million workers—about two-thirds of the total number of manual workers in the industries covered.

4.4.2. *Compilation of the present OES*

The October Earnings Survey is conducted on a voluntary basis by the Department of Employment. The sample of firms for the manufacturing and other industries covered is very large, so that about two-thirds of the manual workers in the relevant industries are surveyed. The figures cover the whole of the United Kingdom.

The numbers covered fluctuate from year to year, but in 1976 about 35,000 establishments gave replies covering about 5 million workers. The information collected relates to one pay week in October, usually towards the beginning of the month. When there has been a stoppage at an establishment during that week, information on a 'normal' week close to the specified pay week is substituted. The enquiry form is a simple one. The only information collected is:

1. The number of the relevant employees at work during the week.
2. The total earnings for that week.
3. The total hours worked in the week.

The total earnings figure is defined to include all bonuses, overtime payments, etc., and before any deductions for income tax or national insurance.

A distinction is made between five separate categories of employee—men, full-time women, part-time women, youths and boys, and girls. Separate information is collected for each of these five groups and for part-time men. The definition used for part-time workers is those ordinarily not employed for more than thirty hours a week. Since the number of women working part-time is considerable separate figures for full and part-time women are given in the published tables. Although statistics for part-time men are collected they are generally excluded from the published statistics since the numbers shown in the returns are insignificant. However, two figures for the hours and average earnings of the small number involved are usually quoted in the annual article.

The data for individual firms are aggregated for each MLH and then for the main SIC Orders. The averages for these groups are calculated by weighting the averages in each individual industry (derived by dividing total earnings by the number of employees) by the estimated total number of manual workers employed in those industries at the latest available date. This procedure mitigates the effect of disparities of coverage in different industries. The industries covered are all manufacturing industries (where coverage is complete), mining and quarrying (except coal), construction, gas, electricity and water, transport and communications (except railways and sea transport), public administration and certain miscellaneous services. The latter consist of laundries and dry cleaning, motor repairers and garages, and repair of boot and shoes. The public administration industry group excludes those industrial employees in national and local government who are included elsewhere in industries such as construction and engineering.

All the earnings figures published in the tables are general averages covering all types of manual workers. Differences in average earnings between industries and regions may be greatly affected by the different proportions of workers of different skills in the work-force. Thus an industry with large numbers of skilled workers may have a higher average earnings figure than one dominated by general labourers, despite the fact that particular grades and occupations in the former industry may be paid less well than similar workers in the latter industry. The importance of these figures is therefore not as an indicator of the relative level of earnings for comparable work in different industries, but as an indicator of changes in absolute levels over time. Or, in the words of the official description . . .

'In view of the wide variations, between different industries, in the proportions of skilled and unskilled workers, in the opportunities for extra earnings from over-time, nightwork and payment-by-results schemes and in the amount of time lost by short-time working, absenteeism, sickness, etc., the differences in average earnings shown in the tables should not be taken as evidence of, or as a measure of, disparities in the ordinary rates of pay prevailing in different industries for comparable classes of workpeople employed under similar conditions.' (*Gazette*, [QRL 24] February 1976, page 132.)

In the published results (see next section for details) figures are given for average hourly earnings. These are calculated from the figures obtained in the enquiry for average weekly earnings and working hours.

4.4.3. *A description of the published results*

The results of the OES are published in an article of about ten pages in the *Gazette* [QRL 24], usually in the February issue. The full results, which are described below, comprise about fifteen tables, with an associated commentary on them, and a description of the survey (see, for instance, *Gazette*, February 1976, pages 131–41).

The format of publication of the results of the OES has remained very much the same for some years. We shall therefore describe the detail available from one particular enquiry, that of October 1975, pointing out any differences in publication that are worth noting. The following tables of results were published in the February 1976 *Gazette* for the second pay week in October 1975:

Table 1. Average weekly earnings, average hours worked, and, average hourly earnings for, (1) all industries covered, and (2) manufacturing industries, for men and women separately, for the latest enquiry, together with similar results for the previous two Octobers.

Table 2. Average weekly earnings by SIC Order for the five groups, listed (full-time men, full-time women, etc.).

Table 3. Average hours worked, as Table 2.

Table 4. Average hourly earnings, as Table 2.

Table 5. Average earnings and hours of full-time men and women, in all industries covered, for a run of seven years.

Table 7. Average weekly earnings and numbers on returns received by MLH for the five specified groups.

Table 8. Average hours worked and average hourly earnings by MLH for the five specified groups.

Table 9. Average weekly earnings (adult males) by region and industry group (Orders of the SIC).

Table 10. Average hours worked, as Table 9.

Table 11. Average hourly earnings, as Table 9.

Tables 12–14. As Tables 9 to 11 but for women aged eighteen and over.

The separate figures for women (Tables 12–14) were not included before October 1974, but have been published in each year since. Table 6, the table missing from the above list, was a table on the earnings and hours of manual workers in the National Health Services. This table gives figures for each of the five groups over the previous three Octobers. These refer to the number of workers on returns, average weekly earnings, average hours worked, and average hourly earnings. This particular table has been a feature of the *Gazette* article since April 1961 when regular enquiries were first started by the Department into earnings and hours of manual employees in hospitals within the National Health Service.These figures are excluded from the summary tables, so that comparability with previous (pre-1961) enquiries is maintained. There is also a difference in the definition of part-time workers—namely, employment involving less than full-time hours—so the figures for National Health Service workers are always shown in a separate table.

Apart from the National Health Services, several other industries are covered at the time of the October enquiry but are not included in the results. Details for coal-mining, agriculture, British Rail, and London Transport are given to the Department and are published in the *Gazette* [QRL 24] but are not regarded as being part of the OES. Prior to October 1974, figures for some of these groups were published with the February *Gazette* article, but since then they have been published separately (see Section 5.2.3.)

4.4.4. *Publication*

The October enquiries are published in the following February issue of the *Gazette* [QRL 24], although industrial action by some of the civil servants involved in compiling the results led to the October 1976 results coming out a month late in the March 1977 *Gazette*. The major article on the enquiry appears once a year (twice yearly before 1970 when the April results were published in the August issue), but the main results are published each month in Table 122 of the *Gazette*.

The table in the *Gazette* gives average weekly and hourly earnings and hours worked by industry group (SIC Order) for full-time men and full-time women for each of the three most recent years. Table 123 gives the same details for manufacturing and all industries for each of the five categories of workers.

A further table, number 125, compares the annual changes in hourly wage earnings derived from the OES with changes in basic hourly wage rates for a period of about fifteen years. A calculation is made to show changes in average hourly wage earnings excluding the effect of overtime, assuming overtime is paid at one and a half times the standard rates. The figure for average hourly wage rates for the same industries is deducted from this to provide a measure of wage drift, though because the earnings and wage rates statistics are constructed in different ways, this is not an exact procedure (see Section 4.1).

Details of the OES also appear in a variety of secondary sources. The *Monthly Digest of Statistics* [QRL 52] gives earnings and hours for the latest nine years by category of worker for all industries covered and for manufacturing industries. The *British Labour Statistics Yearbooks* [QRL 19] contain summary tables providing about five years data by industry group for each of the five categories, and analysing the data jointly by industry and region (Tables 35–8). The *Annual Abstract of Statistics* [QRL 13] gives the same information as the *Monthly Digest* for a run of about ten years. Regional results are given, with differing degrees of emphasis and detail, in the *Abstract of Regional Statistics* [QRL 11], the *Scottish Abstract of Statistics* [QRL 70], the *Scottish Economic Bulletin* [QRL 71], the *Digest of Welsh Statistics* [QRL 26], *Welsh Economic Trends* [QRL 83], and the *Digest of Statistics, Northern Ireland* [QRL 25]. The latter gives average weekly earnings of adult male and female manual workers by industry for over twenty years. It also gives the results of a separate enquiry into the earnings of hourly paid workers for certain occupations in the engineering industry (similar to that described in Section 5.2.1).

The main results of the October (and April) surveys from 1940 to 1968 and of the earlier surveys between 1886 and 1938 are reproduced in *British Labour Statistics; Historical Abstract 1886–1968* [QRL 18].

The material from the post-war surveys has been used by Dean [QRL 3] to derive two series for the earnings of male manual workers in the public and private sectors for the period 1950–76. However, there are great difficulties in such an exercise, since different industries (by MLH) have to be allocated to one or other sector whereas they may straddle both (e.g. transport and communication) or may move between sectors over time (e.g. the steel industry). The resulting series are therefore not ideal, but within the limitations of the data they are probably the best that can be produced. Since 1970 it has been possible to use NES data for such exercises (see Section 4.3), but for the period before 1970 the major source of earnings data is the October (and April) surveys. It was partly because this material was limited to manual workers' earnings that the more comprehensive New Earnings Surveys were introduced. From the point of view of long runs of data on a consistent basis it is nevertheless useful that the October survey has been retained.

CHAPTER 5

EARNINGS—OTHER OFFICIAL SOURCES AND SALARY SURVEYS

5.1. Introduction

We have already described the three major sources of official earnings statistics in the previous section—the monthly index (Section 4.2), the *New Earnings Survey* (Section 4.3) and the *October Earnings Survey* (Section 4.4). In this section we consider a variety of other official earnings statistics (Section 5.2), official statistics on salaries apart from the NES (Section 5.3), and finally the very large number of salary surveys (Section 5.4).

5.2. Other Official Earnings Statistics

5.2.1. *January and June occupational earnings enquiries*

In addition to the enquiry into the earnings of manual workers by industry (OES) and the very detailed NES, there is also an enquiry into earnings by occupation. This is conducted in January and June each year. Its coverage, however, is limited. It is confined to adult male manual workers in a number of industries. Shipbuilding and ship repairing and chemical manufacture are covered in January and June, engineering and some other metal-using industries in June. The latter had been covered in January as well up to and including January 1970. Up to then iron and steel and construction had also been covered but those enquiries were then discontinued. The enquiries were first started in 1963 and are held on a sample basis (although the survey in engineering was a continuation of earlier surveys by the Engineering Employers' Federation). Enquiry forms are sent to all known firms with 500 or more employees, to half the firms with 100 to 499 employees, and to 10 per cent of firms with 25 to 99 employees. Thus in June 1976, for instance, 2,470 firms were required to provide information (under the Statistics of Trade Act, 1947). From these, about 1,970 (80 per cent) returns were received completed and suitable for processing. Information for a specified pay week is collected on:

1. The number of adult male workers.
2. The total hours worked (including overtime).
3. The number of overtime hours.
4. Total gross earnings.
5. The amount of overtime premium payments.

The engineering industries covered by the enquiry are those in Orders VII, IX (part), X (part), XI and XII (part) of the SIC. Only one part of SIC Order X is covered; namely, MLH 370.1, 'shipbuilding and ship-repairing'. In chemicals (SIC Order V), MLH

62

271–3 and 276–8 are covered. The full details of coverage are shown in the *Gazette* [QRL 24] article (see, for instance, October 1976 *Gazette*, page 1132).

The enquiry covers only adult male manual workers and is confined to some broad occupational groups (e.g. fitters). A distinction is made between different types of workers; skilled, semi-skilled, and labourers, and time-workers and payment-by-results workers. Workers not directly involved in production—such as cleaners, canteen staff, and storemen—are excluded. Altogether the results cover about 750,000 workers; some 650,000 in engineering (June) and about 50,000 each in shipbuilding and chemicals (January and June). Definitions of the various terms used in the survey are given in detail in the *Gazette* of October 1974 (pages 903–4), but are fairly standard.

The results are reported in articles in the *Gazette* [QRL 24] which usually appear in the May and October issues (for the January and June enquiries respectively). They also appear in less detail in Table 128 of the *Gazette* and in the *British Labour Statistics Yearbooks* [QRL 19].

The occupations surveyed vary with the particular industry (or MLH) being considered, although the aggregate results (Tables 2–4 in the June 1976 enquiry) are presented for skilled, semi-skilled, and labourers. However, these particular groupings are much broader than those used for categorizing workers at the MLH level. In motor-vehicle manufacturing (MLH 381), for instance, fourteen different classes of workers are distinguished, the classification depending on the exact nature of the work involved and the degree of skill and training. However, all the engineering industries use the same occupational classification so that there is a certain amount of comparability across different industries.

Tables 5–12 (June 1976 enquiry) give estimates of average weekly and hourly earnings and weekly hours in the various occupations in the specified industry groups. The results are given separately for time-workers and PBR workers, and sometimes for all workers. The earnings figures are given first, including overtime premium payments, and then excluding them. The changes from year to year are also given in Tables 2–4. The usual caveats concerning comparisons between industries and over different years are in order. Earnings in the particular pay-week may not be representative of pay over longer periods (especially when overtime pay is included), and the temporal comparisons are not based on matched samples so that changes in earnings will include the effect of labour turnover. Regional results by skill and occupation are given for the standard regions of Great Britain, but Northern Ireland is excluded from the enquiry.

One interesting analysis which is included in these results but is not readily available elsewhere is a classification of occupational earnings in the engineering industries covered by size of firm. The three categories of firms with (*a*) 25–99 employees, (*b*) 100–499 employees, and (*c*) 500 or more employees, are separately analysed. Unfortunately this analysis is not extended to either shipbuilding or chemicals.

A run of results for two or three years is given in Table 128 of the *Gazette* [QRL 24]. However, these figures are given only for the threefold skill classification already described, though separate figures are given for time-workers, PBR workers, and all workers combined. Average weekly earnings including overtime premiums and average hourly earnings excluding overtime premiums are presented, but in an index form with 1964 = 100. However, the latest enquiry results are also given in £ or p so that it is easy enough to calculate the previous years' nominal earnings from the index figures. Prior to 1970 the results for iron and steel manufacture were also provided.

5.2.2. *April enquiry into manual workers' earnings in selected industries*

When the biannual enquiry into manual workers' earnings was changed to an annual (October) enquiry in 1970 (see Section 4.4), the previous April enquiry was continued in a few selected industries. These were industries where there were felt to be 'special needs' which could not be met from the New Earnings Survey. Enquiries were therefore carried out in April 1970, at the request of the industrial organizations concerned, into the following twelve manufacturing and three service industries:

MLH (1968 SIC)	Industry group
213	Biscuits
218	Fruit and vegetable products
229	Food industries not elsewhere specified
261	Coke ovens and manufactured fuel
272	Pharmaceutical chemicals and preparations
362	Insulated wires and cables
383	Aerospace equipment
395	Cans and metal boxes
411	Production of man-made fibres
415	Jute
429	Textile industries not elsewhere specified
431	Leather and fellmongery
893	Dry-cleaning
895	Repairs of boots and shoes
906	Local government service

As a result of the much reduced coverage, forms were issued to only about 3,300 establishments.

The results relate to manual workers only and are given separately for four groups of full-time workers—men aged 21 and over, youths and boys aged under 21, women aged 18 and over, and girls aged under 18. Separate results are given for part-time women workers (those ordinarily employed for less than thirty hours a week). The figures relate to a pay week at the beginning of April and are just like the previous April enquiries and the surviving October enquiries. Employers are asked for the numbers involved, the total gross weekly earnings, and the total hours worked, from which the average hourly earnings are deduced.

The results of this survey are published each year in the August issue of the *Gazette* [QRL 24]. They are published in no other source; they are not regarded as being of much importance (except to the industries concerned) as their coverage is so narrow. Indeed, the coverage is now much less than in April 1970 since four of the original fifteen industries are no longer surveyed. These are food industries not elsewhere specified, production of man-made fibres and local government service (dropped in 1971), and fruit and vegetable products (dropped in 1973). In addition, the jute industry was omitted in 1973, but has been included in all other years. The number of forms sent out has fallen accordingly, from 3,300 in 1970 to 1,500 in 1971 and to 990 in 1976. Indeed the number of firms covered has fallen in each year since the first of these (continuation) enquiries in April 1970, although the response rate of 'usable' forms still remains high at about 90 per cent.

5.2.3. *Earnings of manual workers in certain industries not covered by the OES*

We have already mentioned in Section 4.4.1 that the *October Earnings Survey* excludes, amongst others, agriculture, coal-mining, London Transport, British Railways, and the docks (until they were included in the main survey in 1969). Information on these industries is regularly provided for the Department of Employment by the organization involved and is published in the *Gazette*. This information is not on a precisely comparable basis to that obtained from the Department of Employment enquiry, so is never included in the aggregate OES results. However, up to 1974 the information has sometimes been published in separate tables in the same article as that giving the main OES results. Since 1975 the details for these other industries have always been published separately. The February 1976 *Gazette*, for instance, contains a separate article on the 'Earnings and hours of manual workers in October 1975' (pages 131–41) which gives details of the latest OES; in the same issue (pages 127–8) there are separate sections on earnings in agriculture, London Transport, coal-mining, and British Rail.

Until 1969 figures were also given for *dock workers* who were formerly on daily or half-daily engagements prior to decasualization of dock labour in September 1967. The last separate figures for this group of workers, now covered in the OES under port and inland water transport, were provided by the National Dock Labour Board and were published in the February 1969 *Gazette* [QRL 24]; average weekly earnings for a pay week in April and October each year and for the three-monthly periods April to June and October to December each year were published for the period 1956–67 (February 1969 *Gazette,* page 130).

Information on earnings in *agriculture* is collected from the regular enquiries of the Ministry of Agriculture, Fisheries, and Food and the Department of Agriculture and Fisheries for Scotland. Northern Ireland is not covered. The figures do not relate to a specific pay-week, which might be abnormally affected by the weather, but to half-yearly or yearly periods. The information collected relates to the total earnings of regular whole-time hired agricultural workers, including all overtime, piece-work, bonuses, premiums, and income-in-kind, valued where applicable in accordance with the Agricultural Wages Order. Agriculture, coal-mining and catering (see below) are the only industries where income in kind is taken into account in assessing total earnings. Since the earnings totals are for periods of six months or a year, they include weeks when earnings were lower on account of sickness, holidays, or other absence. In contrast the October earnings enquiry includes only the effects of those who are absent for part of the week. Average weekly hours worked are also collected; they include hours paid for statutory holidays and exclude time lost for any other cause. The results are given for men (20 years and over), youths (under 20), and women and girls.

Statistics on average weekly earnings, average hours worked, and average hourly earnings are calculated. The results are published in the February *Gazette* [QRL 24] (and in the August *Gazette* prior to 1970). Three half-yearly periods are given, and one yearly period. The yearly period is the previous April–March, the half-yearly figures are for the previous two April–September periods and the previous October–March period. A run of ten years' figures is given in the *British Labour Statistics Yearbooks* [QRL 19], as for instance in Table 47 of the 1974 volume. In that table there are also figures for coal-mining, British Rail, London Transport, and the National Health Service.

The information on *coal-mining* is specially provided by the National Coal Board (NCB). It refers to a particular pay week in October each year (and to April as well before 1970). Two sets of figures are recorded; the average weekly earnings excluding the value of allowances in kind, and the value of allowances in kind. These allowances consist mainly of the value of concessionary coal valued at pit-head prices and an element of concessionary rents. The published figures relate to the earnings of adult male workers in the industry in Great Britain. The age at which the adult rate was paid was 21 years until February 1972, 20 years from February 1972, 19 years from April 1973 and 18 years from March 1974. The figures for average weekly earnings include sickness pay and the value of provisions for holidays with pay and rest days. The latter were separately specified as from 1973, whilst sickness pay was also specified as from 1974. Since then the following average earnings figures have therefore been published: cash earnings, sickness pay, the value of provisions for holidays with pay and rest-days, total earnings (equal to the first three combined), and the value of allowances in kind. These figures for the three most recent Octobers are published in the February *Gazette* [QRL 24].

Since the February 1975 issue there has also been a printed warning that

> '. . . the National Coal Board figures are on a different basis from, and so not directly comparable with, the results of the October earnings and hours enquiries carried out by this Department.' (February 1975 *Gazette*, p. 104.)

The origins of this warning lie in the enquiry by the Pay Board into the pay of mineworkers in February 1974 (when the miners' strike was the cause of the calling of a General Election). The comparisons which were being made by some users between the average earnings of coal-miners, based on the NCB figures described above, and the average weekly earnings of manual workers in manufacturing, based on the OES, were shown to be on a different basis. This would have been clear to those who were careful in reading the published descriptions of these figures. The OES figures did not include any element of holiday pay and contained, at most, only a small amount of sick pay, whereas the NCB figures had substantial amounts of both and averaged sick pay over those at work. This particular problem, which is discussed in the Pay Board's *Special Report on the Relative Pay of Mineworkers* [B 43], has become a classic example of the misuse of statistics.

Information on the earnings of manual workers in *British Rail* has been provided by British Rail every spring and autumn since September 1963. From April 1949 to April 1962 earnings figures had been supplied by the British Transport Commission. These results, which related to March or April each year, were published in their *Annual Census of Staff* [QRL 14], with summaries of the results being reported at intervals in the *Gazette* [QRL 24] (e.g. December 1962 issue, page 462). No similar census was taken in the spring of 1963 but the British Railways Board provided details for the week ending 7 September 1963, similar to those collected in the OES. Since then the British Railways Board has regularly provided earnings information each April and October (or in an adjacent month). This information is later published in the *Gazette*.

The figures supplied by the British Transport Commission up till 1962 related to the following workers; railway workshop and conciliation grades (all railway staff excluding officers), ships and marine staff, docks and harbour staff, inland waterways employees, and hotel and catering staff. From 1963 the figures supplied by the British Railways

Board have covered manual workers on the railways and the ships and marine staff. Information on the latter group was published until 1971, but since then only railway grades have been covered. Separate figures are given for workshop staff and wages staff other than workshop, but a combined figure is given for all male adult wages staff. Figures for the small numbers of male juniors, full-time and part-time female adults, and female juniors are also given. The information supplied relates to the numbers involved, their average weekly earnings in the pay-week concerned, and the average hours worked. Those results are published as soon as they are made available at irregular intervals once or twice a year. As an example the February 1977 *Gazette* (page 132) gives details of earnings of British Rail manual workers for the pay-weeks ended 3 April 1976 and 9 October 1976. The previous set of figures had been given in the June 1976 *Gazette* (page 589) for the pay-weeks ended 18 October 1975 and 3 April 1976.

Because the earnings of British Rail Workers are not always published in the same issue of the *Gazette* as the OES results, it is a time-consuming task to run through back numbers of the *Gazette* in order to build up a long time series. Some of the figures are summarized in the *British Labour Statistics Yearbooks* [QRL 19] and the *Historical Abstract* [QRL 18] but since the original source may often have to be located a list of the relevant issues of the *Gazette* since 1963 is given below. The pre-1963 figures supplied by the British Transport Commission are reported in the December 1962 *Gazette* (page 462), where there is a reference to earlier statistics. A long run of data on nationalized industries such as British Rail is given in the *Annual Abstract of Statistics* [QRL 13]. The following *Gazette* [QRL 24] issues provide later British Rail figures: April 1964; January and October 1965; February and October 1966; February and November 1967; February and December 1968; February, September, and December 1970; May and August 1971; June and August 1972; December 1973; April and August 1974; May 1975; February and June 1976; February and July 1977; August 1978; February 1979.

Information on the earnings of manual workers in *London Transport* has been supplied by the London Transport Board (later Executive) since 1963. Earlier figures are available for men only and can be found in *British Labour Statistics; Historical Abstract* [QRL 18], Table 50, for Aprils between 1956 and 1962. Then, from October 1963 and in each April and October thereafter, the earnings figures for London Transport are published in the *Gazette*. The figures are also published in the *Annual Abstract of Statistics* [QRL 13] and the *British Labour Statistics Yearbooks* [QRL 19].

The figures collected relate to the average weekly earnings of manual workers for three groups of staff: road staff, rail staff, and common services. An aggregate figure for all classes is also given. From 1963 to 1976 the earnings were further classified into males, full-time females, and part-time females. Since 1976 separate figures have been given for full-time and part-time men, full-time and part-time women, youths and boys, girls, all males, and all females (see the figures for April 1976 in the June 1976 *Gazette*, page 589). However, the different methods used for compiling figures since 1976 have meant that the new figures are not on a comparable basis to the earlier ones. An attempt to explain the differences and a set of figures for October 1975 and 1976 recalculated on the old basis are given in the July 1977 *Gazette* (page 729). Unless recalculated figures are always given there is likely to be a discontinuity in the series from 1977 onwards.

Publication of these half-yearly figures has also been rather haphazard since the figures are provided rather irregularly. We therefore provide a list of the relevant issues of the *Gazette* in which London Transport earnings have appeared since 1963: April and October 1964; January and October 1965; February and October 1966; February and August 1967; February and August 1968; February and August 1969; February and December 1970; May and August 1971; June and August 1972; April and August 1974; March and July 1975; February and June 1976; February and July 1977; February and August 1978; February and August 1979.

A series of historical statistics for the earnings of manual workers in agriculture, coal-mining, British Rail, inland waterways (up to 1962), London Transport, dock labour, and the National Health Service (from 1961) for April from 1956 to 1968 is given in *British Labour Statistics Historical Abstract* [QRL 18], Table 50. Later figures are given in the *British Labour Statistics Yearbooks* [QRL 19] but the *Gazette* [QRL 24] contains the latest information.

5.2.4. *Earnings in agriculture*

We have already described the information on earnings which is provided alongside the OES in the February issues of the *Gazette* [QRL 24] (see Section 5.2.3). This information, which is collected by a series of regular enquiries, as described below, is supplemented by an article on the hours and earnings of agricultural workers in Great Britain which is regularly published in the October issue of the *Gazette*. The first two of these articles appeared in the September 1963 and September 1964 *Gazettes,* but subsequent articles appeared in October issues with the exception of 1966 and 1978 when they appeared in the November issues of the *Gazette*.

The information collected in these enquiries is a by-product of the work carried out by government officers in ensuring compliance with the Wages Board Orders. These officers are authorized to enter farms and require employers and workers to inform them about wages paid and about hours and conditions of employment. A random sample of about 6,000 farms in Great Britain (orginally 7,000) is covered each year, although specific complaints of underpayment are also investigated. The results for earnings are calculated from the sample enquiries, the randomly selected sample changing from year to year.

An analysis by type of job is made for classifying the results, though only for full-time adult male workers. This analysis by occupation is based on the classification of farm workers by their primary function. Such a classification is inevitably somewhat arbitrary because most workers are engaged on a variety of tasks. The particular jobs isolated are:

1. General farm workers.
2. Foremen and grieves.
3. Dairy cowmen.
4. Other stockmen.
5. Tractor drivers.
6. Horticultural workers.
7. Other farm workers.

For these groups the following results are given:

1. The composition of average weekly earnings, for the year ended the previous 31 March, as between:

    (*a*)   cash and insurance,
    (*b*)   payments-in-kind,
    (*c*)   other earnings.
2. The breakdown of the resulting total earnings between:
    (*a*)   prescribed wage (i.e. as laid down in the Wages Order),
    (*b*)   premium (an addition of 13 per cent on average in 1976).
3. The distribution of weekly earnings for about thirty different earnings ranges for the preceding first quarter and the third quarter of the previous year.
4. Average weekly earnings for the four quarters from the previous April to March period.
5. Average weekly total hours for the same four quarters.
6. Average basic hours and overtime for the year ended the previous 31 March.
7. Payments in kind for all men in the previous year (with no separate categories), England and Wales and Scotland separately. The percentage of workers receiving board and/or lodging, a house, and milk, and the average weekly value of such benefits, is given.

For all these results an average for men is also given, and for 1, 2, 4, 5, and 6, results for youths and for women and girls are given. These results are much more detailed than those given with the OES in the February *Gazette* [QRL 24].

There is also some other information on agricultural earnings in the NES. For agriculture features in the analyses by agreement (the Wage Boards for England and Wales and Scotland), by industry (SIC I), and by occupation (KOS XI). However, the NES information, though very detailed, may suffer from being related to one specified pay-week in April, when seasonal and weather factors may unduly affect earnings.

Besides being published in the *Gazette* the results of the enquiry are summarized in quarterly statements issued by the Ministry of Agriculture and in regular Press Notices. A series of the earnings of agricultural workers for a number of years is given in the *Annual Abstract of Statistics* [QRL 13]. A summary of the main results for 1945–65 was published in 1967 by the Ministry in *The Changing Structure of the Agricultural Labour Force in England and Wales—Numbers of Workers, Hours and Earnings* [QRL 22].

5.2.5. *Earnings of selling staff in retail distribution*

A survey into the earnings and hours of selling staff in retail shops was made by the Department of Employment in May of each year from 1965 to 1968. The survey then ceased because of the advent of the NES. The results of these four enquiries were published in the December issues of the *Gazette* [QRL 24] for the same years. The enquiries related only to those shops with eleven or more employees, thus excluding a large proportion of the total retail staff. Enquiry forms were sent to all known establishments with one hundred or more workers and to a limited number of those in the lower-size range. The information obtained was the average earnings and hours worked by selling-staff in a pay-week in mid May, including separate details for both part-time and 'Saturday-only' workers. Shops were classified into four types: (1) supermarkets; (2) grocery, provision, and other food shops; (3) department and variety stores; and (4) other non-food stores. The definitions of these types of shop are given with the results; for example, in the December 1968 *Gazette*, pages 1005–7.

The results published were as follows:

1. An analysis of the numbers of full-time, part-time, and Saturday-only selling staff by size of shop.
2. Number of establishments and selling staff on the returns by type and size of shop.
3. The numbers, average weekly earnings, average weekly hours, and average hourly earnings for full-time, part-time, and Saturday-only workers, by size of shop and type of shop, and for adult males, youths, boys, adult females, and girls.

Although this survey was discontinued after 1968 because of the NES, the detailed results by size and type of shop were not replaced with the same amount of detail from the NES. This particular survey therefore provides a unique analysis for the four years, 1965–68. The scope of the enquiries was, however, fairly limited, covering only about 200,000 employees out of a total of about 2,000,000 employees employed in the retail distributive trades. From this point of view the NES, though only a 1 per cent sample, has a much more representative coverage of the retail distributive trades than the previous enquiries.

The results of this enquiry for the last three years 1966–68 for those shops with more than one hundred employees are given in British Labour Statistics; Historical Abstract [QRL 18], Table 62. The 1965 results were excluded since the enquiry of that year was a pilot study and was on a slightly different basis (see December 1965 Gazette, pages 528–32). Additional information on the occupations of all persons employed in the retail establishments covered by the earnings enquiries was obtained in 1966, 1967, and 1968. The detailed analysis of this occupational information for May 1968 was published in a separate article in the December 1968 Gazette [QRL 24] pages 997–1004.

5.2.6. Family Expenditure Survey (FES)

Some information on earnings is provided by the Family Expenditure Survey (FES). This source is described in the review in this series on Personal Incomes [B 34] by Stark (Section 3.4) so we shall mention it here only briefly. The FES, which started in January 1957, is a continuous inquiry into the expenditure and income of a changing sample of about 7,000 households in the United Kingdom (apart from 1957 when Northern Ireland was not covered). The results show, amongst other things, how individual members of a household contribute to household income. The main results appear in an annual report by the Department of Employment, entitled the Family Expenditure Survey [QRL 30], which is issued about nine or ten months after the calendar year to which the results refer. Brief results of the latest FES are also given in the June and September issues of the Gazette [QRL 24]. The details of the survey are described in Kemsley's Family Expenditure Survey; Handbook on the Sample, Fieldwork and Coding Procedures [B 22].

The concept of income used in the FES is a broad one.It includes earnings (whether employed or self-employed), some fringe benefits, occupational pensions, income from property and investments, interest on loans, social security benefits and analogous payments from other sources, and education grants and scholarships. Windfall payments such as legacies, gambling winnings, payments from insurance policies, and the sale of assets are ignored. A distinction is made between 'current' income and 'normal' income. Current income refers in most cases to the weekly payment last received, but applies to a longer period of time when payments such as self-employed earnings and income from investments are considered. Since no common reference period is used for these components of current income, the concept of 'normal' income has been developed. The informant is also asked whether the pay he received in the last period was the usual amount, and, if not, he is then asked to give an estimate of his usual or average pay. From this an estimate of the household's normal income is calculated.

The majority of the tables of FES results give details of household size and expenditure patterns, but a few results on the sources of household income are also given. The following seven sources of total average weekly income are isolated:

(a)　Wages and salaries.
(b)　Self-employment—earnings or profits of a trade or business after deduction of business expenses but before deduction of tax.
(c)　Investments—interest from loans, dividends from stocks and shares, income from trusts or covenants, rent from property other than own residence (after deducting allowable expenses), and other unearned income.
(d)　Annuities and occupational pensions.
(e)　Social security benefits.
(f)　Sub-letting and imputed income from owner/rent-free occupancy.
(g)　Other sources.

Details of the average weekly income from these different sources is given for the head of the household, the wife of the head, and other members, to give a total household income. A further analysis of these same sources of income is given by household composition, by household income, by type of administrative area, and by occupation and age of head of household. Until 1971 there was also an analysis of the earnings of employees by range of earnings. This was discontinued because of the similar information being given by the NES, although the figures can still be obtained from the Department of Employment.

The results of the FES are used in examining the effects of taxes and benefits on household income. Articles on this subject have been published in *Economic Trends* [QRL 27] regularly since the early 1960s, usually in an issue at about the turn of the year. From time to time there have also been articles in *Economic Trends* examining the effects of taxes and benefits over a period of years, as, for instance, in R. Harris, 'A review of the effects of taxes and benefits on household incomes 1961–75', *Economic Trends* [QRL 27], January 1977.

The information on earnings provided by the FES is not as detailed as that provided by the NES. But the FES has a broader coverage in that it;

(a)　looks at household rather than individual income, and
(b)　looks at other sources of income apart from the earnings component which we have been examining so far.

5.2.7. *General Household Survey*

The General Household Survey (GHS), like the FES, also provides some information on household incomes. The survey, which is very much like the FES in its sampling techniques, was first conducted in 1971. This survey is also described in the Stark review on *Personal Incomes* [B 34] so we confine ourselves here to a brief description only.

The purpose of the survey is to meet the various needs of many government departments and other users of statistics within one survey. The questions used in the survey therefore cover a very wide range of topics and earnings data are only a very small part of the results. The survey method is exactly the same as the FES; that is, it is a continuous survey covering a changing sample of households. However, the survey is confined to Great Britain, whilst the FES also includes Northern Ireland, and the sample is half as large again as the FES, producing planned samples of about 13,000 households.

The data on incomes are not dealt with in separate sections or tables because the survey is not designed specifically to produce such data. Instead the information is half-hidden in tables on household type, house tenure, size of mortgage payments or rent, participation in selected leisure activities, educational qualifications, and incidence of sickness. Much of this sort of cross-tabulated material will be of more use in testing of hypotheses about economic and social behaviour than in studies of income *per se*. But it is a valuable data source, nevertheless, for this sort of information is available from no other source. The questions are less detailed than in the FES, however, so that the results may be less accurate.

The concept of income is slightly different from the 'current' and 'normal' income employed in the FES. As far as possible a concept of gross cash income received over the preceding twelve months (prior to interview) is used. Such incomes are defined to include earnings from employment and self-employment, transfers of all kinds, and net investment and property incomes. The incomes of all the household members aged over sixteen are obtained, household income being the sum of these individual incomes. The weekly income is calculated by dividing the total income by fifty-two. Weekly earnings are also established by finding out the earnings received in the previous twelve months and dividing by fifty-two. Employment and self-employment earnings are separately established.

The first survey, conducted in 1971, was published in 1973 in the Office of Population Censuses and Surveys' *The General Household Survey; Introductory Report* [QRL 35]. Subsequent volumes have been published by the same body in each year since then in *The General Household Survey* [QRL 34]. A review article by F. R. Oliver on the initial survey, entitled 'The General Household Survey' [B 30], gives a succinct account of the GHS and a critical assessment of its usefulness and possible development.

5.2.8. *Department of Health and Social Security data*

The Department of Health and Social Security has some interesting information on earnings which arises as a by-product of the State Graduated Pension Scheme which was introduced in April 1961. Graduated contributions are recorded on deduction cards which also record gross annual taxable earnings. A sample of these records is drawn in order to analyse the earnings information that they provide. Results are tabulated by sex, age, marital status, and region for those contributors known to be in employment for the whole year. A fuller description of the sampling procedures used and the presentation of the results is given in Whitehead's review of 'Social security statistics' [B 35], pages 11–13. These data are especially useful for statistics on earnings by age and by region.

The statistics from this survey were first produced in 1964–5 and have been produced in every year since. The results are published in the *Abstract of Regional Statistics* [QRL 11], the *Scottish Abstract of Statistics* [QRL 70] and the *Digest of Welsh Statistics* [QRL 26]. However, the Department clearly has much more material on earnings than is published in those sources and this is sometimes available on request.

5.2.9. *Survey of Personal Incomes*

The Survey of Personal Incomes is a random sample of tax records instituted by the Inland Revenue. The main purpose of the survey is to assess the yield of taxes and their impact on different groups, but an important by-product is the information which is provided on earnings. The survey has been carried out annually since 1962/3 but there were earlier surveys at intervals of about five years. The first of these surveys was conducted before the war. Then in the post-war period, there were major samples of about 1,000,000 tax records in 1949/50 and at five-year intervals up until the 1969/70 survey. After that, the smaller annual survey, with a sample of about 100,000 to 150,000 tax records, was regarded as sufficient and the larger sample was discontinued. The survey is discussed in the May 1972 issue of *Statistical News* [QRL 73] and is fully described in the *Survey of Personal Incomes, 1969/70* [QRL 79]. Until 1966/7 the results were published in the *Annual Reports of the Board of Inland Revenue* [QRL 15]; the 1967/8 and 1968/9 results were published in *Inland Revenue Statistics* [QRL 44]. Since then the results have been published in a separate report on the *Survey of Personal Incomes* [QRL 79]. There is, however, a publication lag of two to three years.

The concept of income used in the survey is that defined for tax purposes. It is therefore a broader definition than the earnings being considered in this review. The main interest of the survey in the present context is that it is the only source of earnings by marital status and by socio-economic group. A certain amount of regional data is also published.

5.2.10. *Census of Production data on earnings*

The Census of Production provides a limited amount of information on wages and salaries for manufacturing industries, mining and quarrying and gas, electricity and water in the United Kingdom. Although censuses were taken roughly every five years from 1907 until 1968, it was not until 1948 that information on wages and salaries became available. Each establishment covered by the census was required to give the average number of persons employed during the year of return (split in later censuses into operatives and other employees) and the wages and salaries paid (similarly split in later censuses). Wages and salaries are defined to include all overtime payments, bonuses, and commissions whether paid regularly or not. The value of any payment in kind, lodging allowance, etc., is excluded and no deduction is made for income tax, national insurance, or pension contributions. Changes over time in the Standard Industrial Classification make it difficult to construct historical series on a consistent basis, but a *Historical Record of the Censuses of Production* [QRL 37] published in

1977, brings together the data in the censuses of production 1907–70 on to the basis of the 1968 Standard Industrial Classification. The data are analysed by industry.

For 1970 and later years censuses have been conducted annually. Preliminary information, by SIC Order, is published around a year after the reference year in *Business Monitor, PA 1000, Census of Production, Provisional Results* [QRL 20]. Final results giving greater industrial and other detail—for example, analyses by size of establishment— are published in individual industry *Business Monitors* [QRL 20]. The full results appear with a lag of three or four years in the *Report on the Census of Production* [QRL 59]. Separate wages and salaries figures are presented for operatives and 'others', where 'others' are defined as administrative, clerical, and technical workers, and operatives as the rest of the employees. Total employment figures for industries include working proprietors. Since employment figures and wages and salaries figures are given on the same basis in the same table, average per capita figures can be calculated. Results for wages and salaries are also broken down by size of establishment. The number of size groupings distinguished within an industry, which ranges from two to nine, depends on the number of establishments within that industry and the confidentiality provisions of the Statistics of Trade Act, 1947. Figures of wages and salaries should not be compared directly across industries because of differences in the structure of the workforce between industries.

Figures for wages and salaries are also presented for enterprises, which are groupings of establishments under common ownership, and are published in millions of pounds by industry and SIC Order in the summary tables, *Business Monitor, PA 1002* [QRL 20].

The material published in the *Census of Production* [QRL 59] on earnings is limited to the wages and salaries figures so described. But since the information is given for nearly all the minimum list headings it provides a rich source of earnings statistics by industry. However, the material has been little used by researchers in the earnings field. This may be because the publication lag for the final results is rather long, but also because the changes in the labour force make comparisons over time or across industries rather difficult.

5.2.11. *Earnings data from enquiries into distribution*

Censuses of distribution were taken for 1950, 1957, 1961, 1966, and 1971, those for 1957 and 1966 being in the nature of sample surveys. Information on wages and salaries was collected in all five censuses but one total figure only was asked for in respect of all persons engaged in each retail or service trade organization as a whole and there is no establishment (i.e. shops) analysis of earnings, nor are earnings analysed by employees according to status. The figures exclude payments (including payments in kind) to owners working in the business as well as to any of their relatives who are not in receipt of a definite wage. No deductions are made, however, for income tax, national insurance, or pensions contributions.

For the retail trades, figures are shown for the numbers of full- and part-time employees and their full-time equivalent. The average wages per head of employees can be calculated separately for co-operative societies, multiples, and independents and for the different kinds of business of multiples and independents (although the establishments of co-operative societies were classified to individual kinds of business, co-operative societies as organizations were not so broken down). Figures of wages and salaries are not shown in size analyses for either the retail or service trades. These results are shown in the *Report on the Census of Distribution* [QRL 58].

From 1976 onwards the censuses of distribution are being replaced by annual Retail Enquiries in which questions on wages and salaries and certain other matters will be included from time to time. They are not included, however, in the 1976 and 1977 questionnaires.

5.3. Official Statistics on Salaries apart from the NES

5.3.1. *Introduction*

In this section we deal with those official sources of statistics on salaries apart from the NES (Section 4.3), which of course has a full coverage of the earnings of non-manual workers. In this context (as throughout this review) we are talking about salaries as being one form of earnings, which is why the NES and the sources which will be described here were not included in the chapter on salary scales (Chapter 3).

Until the advent of the full NES in 1970 there had been a regular enquiry each year since 1955 into the earnings of administrative, technical, and clerical employees. It was also used in calculating an index of salaries. This enquiry and its associated index are described in Section 5.3.2. The enquiry was superseded by the NES in 1970 and was therefore dropped; the new index of salaries, based on NES data, which was then introduced, is described in Section 5.3.3. However, as from 1973, a new enquiry into the earnings of non-manual employees was initiated (at the request of the EEC) and this is described in Section 5.3.4.

5.3.2. *Earnings of administrative, technical, and clerical employees, 1955–70*

In 1955 the then Ministry of Labour introduced a new enquiry into the earnings of administrative, technical, and clerical employees in the public sector (including the utilities), banking and insurance. Something like 2,000,000 salaried employees were covered by this enquiry, which was virtually all of those in the relevant groups. In October 1959 this enquiry was extended to the rest of the production industries—to manufacturing, mining, and quarrying other than coal, water supply, and construction. These enquiries were then held every year up to October 1970, after which they were dropped because of the extensive coverage of white-collar workers by then being provided by the NES (see Appendix V of *New Earnings Survey 1968* [QRL 55], pages 190–3).

The original 1955 enquiry covered the earnings of male and female administrative, technical, and clerical employees in national and local government, education (teachers), the National Health Service, insurance and banking, and the nationalized industries (coal, gas, electricity, British Rail, British Transport Docks, British Waterways, and air transport). The information from these sectors was collected on a voluntary basis and was extended to London Transport in 1963 and British Road Services in 1966.

The additional industries included in 1959 were required to provide the same information on male and female earnings under the Statistics of Trade Act, 1947. The Ministry of Commerce in Northern Ireland collected information for Northern Ireland under the Statistics of Trade Act (Northern Ireland) 1949.

Information was collected for monthly-paid and weekly-paid employees separately, but it should be borne in mind that firms have different practices as to their payment methods so undue weight should not be given to this distinction. It is therefore probably wiser to look at the figures for monthly-paid and weekly-paid combined, on a weekly basis.

The usual warning about comparing absolute levels of pay between different groups of workers applies and is worth repeating;

'. . . when considering information for separate industry groups it should be remembered that because of the variations between industries in the proportions of adults and young persons, and of highly qualified staff and routine office workers, the difference in the average earnings in the tables cannot be taken as evidence of, or as a measure of, disparities in ordinary rates of salary prevailing in different industries for comparable classes of employee working under similar conditions' (April 1971 *Gazette* [QRL 24], page 355).

In the public sector, the coverage of organizations in the enquiry was virtually complete. In the production industries, only firms with 25 or more employees (including all workers) were covered. Forms were sent to all known firms with 100 or more employees and to 50 per cent of all known firms with 25 to 99 employees. The firms in this smaller size range accounted (after grossing up) for between 5 and 10 per cent of the aggregate figures in the tables. In the early years of the enquiry about 20,000 forms were sent out each year. By the time of the last enquiry in 1970, some 17,500 forms were sent out to firms in Great Britain with 15,000 being returned suitable for tabulation. In the production industries about 2,000,000 out of a total of 2,500,000 salaried employees were covered by the enquiry.

Employers were asked for the numbers of the relevant employees, monthly-paid and weekly-paid separately, and the total salaries for the month of October or for a specified pay-week in October paid to each group. A distinction was made between males, full-time females, and part-time females. Salaries were taken to include all overtime payments, bonuses, commissions, etc., i.e. the same payments as the previous definition of earnings. Where bonuses or commissions were paid at longer intervals than monthly or weekly, employers were asked to include in the earnings an appropriate proportionate amount for the period of the return.

The results of this enquiry were published in the *Gazette* [QRL 24] in March each year between 1962 and 1970. The first two enquiries, for October 1959 and October 1960, were published somewhat later, in September 1960 and June 1961 respectively. Also the last enquiry, for October 1970, was published a month later in the April 1971 *Gazette*, following delays in the return of the questionnaire due to a national postal dispute. The October 1969 enquiry was published in two forms; first, in March 1970 using the 1958 SIC, and second, in September 1970 using the revised 1968 SIC. This change of classification made insignificantly small differences to the majority of the results (see September 1970 *Gazette*, pages 784–7).

In the latter years the following five tables were published:

Table 1. Average earnings and numbers covered by industry group (production industries only); males and females separately.

Table 2. The same, with full-time and part-time females separately.

Table 3. Indices of male and female average earnings in certain industries:

(*a*) national and local government including teachers and National Health Service.

(*b*) nationalized industries.

(*c*) insurance and banking.

Table 4. Average earnings of clerical and analogous employees and of all employees in Table 3; males and females separately.

Table 5. Numbers covered, average earnings, and indices of all employees in all industries and services covered by the enquiry; males and females separately, plus an index for all employees (October 1959 = 100).

The combined results for the production industries and public administration and certain other services (shown in Table 5) covered something like 4,500,000 employees by 1970.

In earlier years, from 1962 up to 1966, the results of the enquiry for the production industries were published separately in the March issues of the *Gazette* already mentioned. These results were then combined with those for public administration and certain other services and published in an article a few months later. The first of these articles in the July 1962 *Gazette* (page 264) introduced the combined results and described the new *index of average salaries* which was now produced. Later articles giving additional salaries data in this same form appeared in issues of the *Gazette* in June 1963, May 1964, May 1965, and April 1966. Then, as from the March 1967 *Gazette*, which reported the October 1966 enquiry, the results were combined in the one article, rather than being published in the two separate articles.

The index of average salaries, with a base of 1959 = 100, is described in an article in the July 1962 *Gazette* [QRL 24]. Figures for the public sector groups are given for the period starting from the first enquiry in 1955, but the index only becomes comprehensive in 1959 when it is possible to include the production industries as well. The main industries and services that are then not represented in the returns are: agriculture, forestry and fishing; privately engaged persons in professions such as accountancy, law, medical, and dental services; finance houses and building societies; miscellaneous services such as entertainment, catering, etc., and the distributive trades.

Separate indices are given for males and females. These indices are current-weighted; they therefore reflect not only the natural growth in earnings but also structural changes in the composition of the work-force—for instance, the increasing numbers of part-time workers and women through the period. However, it has been estimated that, by the end of the eleven-year period 1959–70, during which time average salaries doubled, an index based on fixed weights (for males and females) would have been only about 1 per cent higher than the published current weighted index (see *Gazette*, May 1972, page 431). The averages for the SIC Orders are also calculated as current-weighted averages of the MLH figures, so that this problem also arises at the industry level (and arises within firms as well).

As well as being reported in regular articles in the *Gazette*, the earnings of administrative, technical, and clerical employees also featured in Tables 123–5 of the statistical series section of the *Gazette* (which started in May 1966 when the format of the *Gazette* was substantially changed). Table 123 gave these earnings for males and females by industry group and for all industries and services from 1960. Table 124 gave the index of average earnings of salaried employees for all industries and services covered since 1955 (with 1959 = 100) for males, females, and all employees. This index for all employees was also reproduced in Table 129 alongside the figures for wage rates and earnings of manual workers. Table 125 gave the average earnings of clerical and analogous employees and all salaried employees in the non-manufacturing industries and services covered by the original enquiry.

A summary of these figures is given for the period 1955–68 or 1959–68 in the *British Labour Statistics; Historical Abstract* [QRL 18], Tables 53, 54, and 85. A comparison with the average earnings of manual workers for the period 1959–68 is given in the same volume, Table 55. This is a series which is described and extended up to 1971 in an article in the May 1972 *Gazette*, pages 431–4. That article also describes a new index on salaries which was developed with the advent of the New Earnings Survey. With the development of this new index, which had the great advantage of being based on fixed weights (though only at industry level), the previous *Gazette* Tables 123–5 and 129 disappeared, to be replaced by two new tables on the earnings of manual workers and by a table on the new index of average salaries (Table 124). The development of this new index is described below.

5.3.3. *The new index of average salaries*

The ending of the enquiries into the earnings of administrative, technical, and clerical employees after 1970 provided an opportune moment for revising the index of salaries. The deficiencies of the old index, based on current weights, were clear to compilers and users alike, so the advent of the full-scale *New Earnings Survey* in April 1970 and the phasing out of the old salaries enquiry in October 1970 provided a double reason for change.

The new index of salaries was introduced in the May 1972 *Gazette* [QRL 24] (pages 431–4) and began to be published in the new Table 124 from the same date. The new index, based on the fuller information provided by the *New Earnings Survey* [QRL 55], has a greater coverage than the previous enquiry since it covers all non-manual employees in all sizes of establishment in all industries and services. The new series also uses fixed weights—namely, the relative numbers of the male and female non-manual employees in the *New Earnings Survey 1970*—in calculating the average earnings of all non-manual employees.

This new index can only be linked to the old series if:

1. The old series is recalculated on fixed weights.
2. One assumes that the movement of the average earnings of all non-manual employees in the earlier years (1959–70) was in line with the movement of the average earnings of those covered by the October enquiries.

The latter assumption is not ideal, but for lack of better information it was nevertheless made by the Department in arriving at the index in Table 124, which ran continuously from 1959 into the 1970s (in issues of the *Gazette* prior to January 1976). The recalculation of the old series using fixed (1970) weights rather than the current weights previously employed, made a difference of about 1 per cent to the index over the period 1959–70. The fixed weight series was derived by using the April 1970 NES proportions of non-manual males and females (0.515 and 0.485 respectively). However, in so far as there were major changes in industrial composition or in the proportion of part-time workers, the new fixed-weight index achieves only part of the necessary 'correction', albeit the most important part. The new (fixed weight) and old (current weight) series are shown in Table 1 of the introductory article in the May 1972 *Gazette* [QRL 24], pages 431–4. Since then only the fixed weight series has been calculated.

An additional link had to be made between the old (fixed-weight) index and the new index to produce a continuous series. The new index related to April each year whilst the old index referred to October. The April 1970 figure on the old series basis was therefore estimated by interpolation between the October 1969 and October 1970 figures, for non-manual males and females separately, using the monthly index of average earnings. This procedure is not ideal since the monthly index covers all workers, manual and non-manual, and both males and females. Nevertheless a certain amount of *ad-hoc* adjustment is necessary when linking any two series. Unfortunately, this particular piece of series-linking is not well 'signposted' in the *Gazette* table, being confined to the brief footnote that the fixed-weight indices are described in the May 1972 issue of the *Gazette*.

There are two other major respects, apart from coverage, in which the new series differs from the old. First, the former series was based on a fairly comprehensive enquiry of the industries concerned whereas the new series, using NES data, is based on a 1 per cent random sample. On this ground alone exact correspondence between the new and old series is not to be expected. But, secondly, the new series refers to Great Britain only whereas the old series covered Northern Ireland as well.

The information provided in the new *Gazette* Table 124 from May 1972 up to the end of 1975 was as follows—an index of average salaries for: (*a*) all industries, (*b*) all manufacturing industries, for the following three groups; non-manual males, non-manual females, and all non-manual employees.

From January 1976 a revised index of salaries began to be published. The need for a revised index arose because of the reduced coverage of part-time and juvenile employees in the NES as from April 1975 (see Section 4.3.2). It was therefore decided to publish the index for non-manual full-time adult employees only. The weights used are of course different from those previously used (0.575 for men and 0.425 for women) and the series can only be taken back to April 1970, but the method of calculation is the same. The data used are the average weekly earnings of all full-time non-manual adult employees whose pay for the survey period was not affected by absence. The new series was introduced in the January 1976 *Gazette* [QRL 24] (page 187) and is published in the once more revised Table 124. The new table gives details of the average salaries of full-time adults, men and women separately and then combined, for all industries and all manufacturing industries, with April 1970 = 100.

5.3.4. *New enquiry into the earnings of non-manual employees in production industries*

A new series of enquiries into the earnings of full-time non-manual employees in the industries covered by the index of production was started in October 1973. The new enquiry, which was introduced only three years after the previous enquiry had been declared redundant with the advent of NES, arose from an EEC request. The United Kingdom was asked to supply information in respect of October each year for a system of harmonized statistics compiled by the Statistical Office of the European Communities. Data for manual workers were already available from the regular October earnings enquiries (see Section 4.4). The new surveys were introduced to provide comparable information for non-manual workers.

The information for October 1973 was obtained as part of the detailed labour costs surveys (see Section 6.3), the results of which were published in the September and October 1975 issues of the *Gazette* [QRL 24]. The October 1974 figures were collected in a separate enquiry which is repeated annually although on a smaller scale than the previous 'salaries' enquiries (see Section 5.3.2).

The enquiries are carried out in Great Britain by the Department of Employment under the Statistics of Trade Act, 1947, and in Northern Ireland by the Department of Manpower Services (DMS) there. They are conducted on an enterprise or company basis, with firms in more than one industry being asked to complete separate returns for each. All firms with 500 or more employees (manual and non-manual) are covered, 25 per cent of those with 100–499 employees, and 10 per cent of those with 50–99 employees. Thus firms with less than 50 employees are excluded from the enquiry. Altogether some 5,000 firms are approached compared with the 17,500 firms covered by the last of the former 'salaries' surveys in October 1970. Of the 5,000 firms covered, returns from something like 95 per cent of them are received in a suitable form for tabulation (a much higher proportion than with the previous surveys). The results for each size-range are grossed up by the appropriate sampling fractions to produce averages for each industry (Minimum List Heading of the Standard Industrial Classification) covered by the enquiry. These industry estimates are weighted together to obtain estimates for each of the industry groups, for all manufacturing industries, and for all industries covered by the survey. The weights used are estimates of the total numbers of non-manual employees in the various industries. These are obtained by applying estimates of the proportions of non-manual employees, obtained from employment surveys, to total numbers of employees in employment in each of the industries shown by the censuses of employment in Great Britain and Northern Ireland. The number of employees covered by the enquiries (after grossing-up by the sampling fractions) is just over 2,000,000.

This weighting method is analogous to that used in the Department's annual October survey of the earnings of manual workers and differs from that used in earlier years for non-manual workers, where the weights, in effect, were the grossed-up numbers covered by the enquiry. However, the results for 1973, 1974, and 1975 have been recalculated using the revised method of weighting and these are available on request from the Department of Employment, Statistics Division C3, Orphanage Road, Watford, Herts.

The information obtained in the enquiry relates to the total earnings for the last pay-week in October (weekly-paid) or for the whole month of October (monthly-paid). All earnings are converted to a .weekly basis to produce figures for average weekly earnings. Salaries paid for holidays, sickness, or training courses during the period are included, but bonuses and commissions paid only periodically (not regularly each week or month) are excluded, even if paid in the October period concerned. It should be noted that, although overtime payments, bonuses, etc., are included, they are not distinguished separately. Hence, the possible effect of any changes in these payments on earnings levels cannot be estimated. Nor is information sought about hours of work.

The non-manual employees covered include directors (unless paid by fee only), managers, superintendents, works or general foremen, professional, scientific and design employees, draughtsmen and tracers, sales representatives, and office employees. Those excluded are managerial staff paid predominantly by a share of profits, working proprietors, and employees working overseas.

The industries covered are all those which are included in the index of industrial production—that is, all manufacturing industries, mining and quarrying, construction and gas, electricity and water.

The results of the first two enquiries, October 1973 and October 1974, were published in the December 1975 *Gazette* [QRL 24], pages 1274–5. The October 1975 enquiry was published in the July 1976 *Gazette*, pages 734–5, and that for October 1976 in the September 1977 *Gazette*, pages 976–7.

The results relating to full-time non-manual employees are published separately for males and females. As in other surveys the definition of full-time in this survey is an employee normally working more than thirty hours a week excluding main meal breaks and overtime.

Average weekly earnings are given for the twenty SIC Orders covered and for all manufacturing industries and all production industries covered. The 1973 and 1974 figures referred to the United Kingdom but in 1975 they refer to Great Britain only as the DMS in Northern Ireland was unable to conduct its own enquiry. However, according to the Department, the differences between the United Kingdom and Great Britain in the October 1974 results were negligible, so that the October 1975 results can 'be regarded as applying to the United Kingdom as a whole' (July 1976 *Gazette*, page 734). Such a procedure is not to be recommended generally but would seem to be sensible in this particular case.

The differences in average earnings between different industries and between males and females should not be regarded as unduly significant. The composition of the labour force may vary from industry to industry and the types of jobs done by men and women may be very different. The Department therefore warns that,

'. . . the difference in average earnings among the industry groups cannot therefore be taken as a measure of disparities in ordinary scales of salary prevailing in different industries for comparable classes of employee working under similar conditions,'

and also that,

'. . . the average salary for males . . . (is) much higher than that for females. . . . However, that does not mean that men and women with similar qualifications and responsibilities received widely different remuneration. For example the women might be doing different types of work and a higher proportion might be engaged on more routine duties; there could also be differences in ages and in the amount of overtime worked.' (*Gazette* [QRL 24], December 1975, page 1274.)

5.4. Salary Surveys

In this section we first discuss the very large number of salary surveys which exist and their advantages and disadvantages (Section 5.4.1). We then look in detail at one particular survey, *Reward* [QRL 66], which has a rather larger coverage than any of the other salary surveys (Section 5.4.2).

5.4.1. *Salary surveys*

The number of salary surveys conducted by various organizations in the United Kingdom is surprisingly large. In 1977 there were about fifty different surveys known to the author but since many of these surveys are privately conducted and little advertised this is probably an underestimate. The quality of these surveys varies enormously from survey to survey so a general warning is perhaps necessary. The user must be very careful to find out exactly what has been measured and how, since some of the information in these surveys is collected in a most unscientific fashion.

Most of the surveys involve some sort of sampling procedures. However, in few cases are these procedures sufficiently accurate for much weight to be given to the results. The sample is often an inaccurate representation of the parent population in two respects:

1. The sample is often so small that the standard error of the results is unsatisfactorily high.
2. The sample is often not selected at random; this is especially true for 'in-house' surveys of members' salaries. Even when the sample is randomly selected the differential response rate often introduces a bias.

In this section, we confine ourselves largely to listing the sources of these surveys and their availability. In some cases the results are available to anyone, although they are often extremely expensive to purchase. We shall also give a brief description of the coverage and content of each survey and will point out any obvious drawbacks which exist. These criticisms will, however, be fairly limited so that the advice must again be repeated that these surveys should be treated with some circumspection.

Given that the salary surveys tend to be a little suspect, is it worth bothering with them at all? The answer is that one of the reasons why the surveys exist is because there has been a gap in the coverage of other salary statistics and hence there is felt to be a need for them. The official index of average salaries, described in Sections 5.3.2 and 5.3.3 is too all-embracing; an index which includes both typists and managing directors gives one little indication of how salaries for particular occupations may be moving. The New Earnings Survey (Section 4.3) gives a fine occupational breakdown but does not pretend to give information on the earnings of those with specific professional qualifications or particular responsibilities. In the public sector, it is possible to find the rates of pay for different classes of employees, although some searching around may be needed. Some information on private-sector workers is also available in publications such as IDS reports and the NALGO data (Section 4.2.1). But generally speaking the coverage of salary statistics is poor. This has led to the demand for the information provided by salary surveys and the rapid growth of these surveys in recent years.

About ten years ago one could count the numbers of such surveys on the fingers of one hand. Now there is a vast number and more appear each year. This growth in such surveys can be partly explained by two factors; first, the growth of white-collar employment over the last twenty years (see Elliott's 'The growth of white-collar employment in Great Britain 1951–1971' [B 9]), and secondly, the additional attention paid to earnings because of the acceleration in inflation and the greater militancy of workers generally. It may also be true that particular articulate white-collar organizations have tended to want information about their own relatively small groups of members for bargaining purposes.

In assessing the usefulness of any of the surveys it is sensible to start by finding out what sort of survey it is. We have already mentioned one type, what we called the 'in-house' survey produced by a professional institute or a trade association. Such surveys are usually carried out by a postal questionnaire sent out to the members. The classification of status or qualifications is consequently subjective and the declaration of earnings may possibly be biased. Furthermore, it is by no means certain that the response rate will be the same across different ages, earnings, or levels in the hierarchy. Some of these surveys are available only to the members of the organization conducting the survey.

A second type of survey is that compiled by consultants or other bodies who specialize in this sort of work. Generally speaking, they have a certain number of client companies who participate in regular surveys of salaries within their organizations. These results are then made known to the participants and may also be sold outside this group. Since the companies themselves are providing the information there is perhaps less risk of wrongly assessing the job status of employees, although differences in job designation between companies may prove confusing. Such surveys may produce much more detailed information on the pay for particular jobs, and companies may also provide information on fringe benefits, etc., which do not appear in other surveys. However, the companies which take part in these surveys are usually large organizations. There may therefore be a bias in the results due to the exclusion of the employees of small firms from the survey.

The other major type of survey is that based on some form of register, usually one for job applicants. Such surveys, compiled from these registers, are bound to be biased. Persons seeking jobs in a particular profession or occupation will not be a representative sample of the population in that group. Furthermore, the information they supply will inevitably be subjective. Job applicants may tend to overstate their present or past salary. On the other hand, they may be persons who are not doing well in their present jobs or who are not successful enough to arrange new jobs. Whilst the overstatement of salary would clearly lend an upward bias to the results, the other factors would clearly impart a downward bias. Over all one imagines that the bias would be downwards. A further factor which should be noted is that surveys of registrants must necessarily be made over some months. In times of inflation this may lead to distortion in the results.

One important tact which we have not mentioned so far in respect of these surveys is the concept of earnings which they measure. This varies between surveys so it is important that the user should be able to establish what the results are showing. In some surveys basic salaries are recorded; in others total remuneration is given. The distinction between these two is not always made clear in surveys. This is unfortunate because the difference between the two may be very important. The listing or valuation of fringe benefits is given in few of the surveys. In fact information on fringe benefits is generally very difficult to obtain (see Section 6.2). However, in several surveys it is not the basic salary of the individual which is collected but the total gross earnings, including bonuses, commission, overtimé, etc., or the average earnings in the year (which may include periods on different salary scales). These are factors which must be established before any of this survey information is used.

One of the critical factors in the usefulness of any survey is the design of the questions. One very rarely finds a questionnaire which is unambiguous in every respect, although the official earnings surveys already described in Chapter 4 tend to be fairly good. It would be useful, but it is rarely the case, if the actual questionnaire used was appended to the report of the results.

A certain looseness in wording is a common feature of most of the private surveys which are listed below.

An excellent guide to the various salary surveys is provided by an annual publication produced by Incomes Data Services Ltd. IDS). In January each year since 1969 they have devoted one of their IDS studies to this subject (see Section 3.2.2). The *IDS Guide to Salary Surveys* [QRL 39] provides a guide to all the major private and institutional surveys. Recent issues have run to thirty-two pages and have given detailed descriptions of these surveys. This source is recommended to users since the guide is revised each year to keep it up to date and it inevitably contains more information than the listing we provide below.

The bare details of the surveys are now listed. The surveys are classified by main occupational headings. The survey organization is named together with details of coverage, the source of the data, and the frequency of the report. Further information is best sought from the *IDS Guide to Salary Surveys* [QRL 39] or from the organization involved. Although the addresses of these organizations are not given here, the reader may assume that they are based in London, unless another city or town is indicated.

LIST OF SALARY SURVEYS

ACCOUNTANTS
   Accountancy Personnel Limited.
        Frequency: twice annually.
        Coverage: accountants and insurance personnel.
        Data source: monitoring by managers of several branches, in major cities of salaries being offered by local companies.
   Computer Economics Ltd.
        Frequency: annually. First report 1976.
        Coverage: top staff in accountancy and personnel.
        Data source: sample of 4,000 individuals in about 150 organizations.
   Lloyd Executive Incomes Research Unit.
        Frequency: annually. First report 1974.
        Coverage: accountants and other financial personnel.
        Data source: sample of 150 firms/5,000 individuals.

ADVERTISING
   Institute of Practitioners in Advertising.
        Frequency: annually.
        Coverage: various advertising functions.

Data source: 280 member firms with about 14,000 staff, and about 50 per cent response.

ARCHITECTS

Royal Institute of British Architects.
>*Frequency*: yearly since 1976. Triennially 1964–76.
>*Coverage*: architects.
>*Data source*: 3,000 members of Institute in work.

BANKING

Lloyds Executive Incomes Research Unit.
>*Frequency*: annually. First report in 1966.
>*Coverage*: professional, executive, and clerical employees, in city banks.
>*Data source*: varying numbers of participating banks.

London Banks' Personnel Management Group.
>*Frequency*: annually. First report in 1974.
>*Coverage*: middle and general grades in banking.
>*Data source*: 85 participating members.

National Union of Bank Employees.
>*Frequency*: irregular.
>*Coverage*: scales of pay, all staff in British banks, some other institutions.
>*Data source*: direct information from fourteen banks, two building societies.

BIOLOGISTS

The Institute of Biology.
>*Frequency*: triennially since 1953.
>*Coverage*: professionally qualified biologists.
>*Data source*: 2,500 members of the Institute.

BUSINESS GRADUATES

The Business Graduates Association.
>*Frequency*: irregularly.
>*Coverage*: graduates of certain business schools.
>*Data source*: 800 members of the association.

BUYERS

The Institution of Buyers.
>*Frequency*: annually, first report in 1976.
>*Coverage*: buyers.
>*Data source*: 6,000 members of the Institution.

CATERING STAFF

The Industrial Society.
>*Frequency*: about once a year.
>*Coverage*: catering staff in industry and company offices.
>*Data source*: 150 organizations.

CHEMISTS
 Royal Institute of Chemistry.
  Frequency: full census triennially since 1973, sample surveys in intermediate
  years since 1953. First remuneration survey in 1919.
  Coverage: professionally qualified chemists.
  Data source: 3,000 members of the Institute.

COMPUTER STAFF
 Computer Economics Ltd.
  Frequency: twice yearly since 1968.
  Coverage: all types of computer staff.
  Data source: 350 organizations employing 18,000 staff.
 Computer Users' Year Book.
  Frequency: annually since 1971.
  Coverage: all types of computer staff.
  Data source: 1,200 organizations employing 22,000 staff.

ECONOMISTS
 Society of Business Economists.
  Frequency: irregularly.
  Coverage: business economists.
  Data source: 230 members of the society.

ENGINEERS
 Council of Engineering Institutions.
  Frequency: biennially since 1971. Earlier surveys, conducted with Ministry of
  Technology in 1966 and 1968, published by HMSO.
  Coverage: professional engineers in fifteen chartered institutes, plus technician
  engineers since 1977.
  Data source: 31,000 members of chartered institutions and, since 1977, a sample
  of 3,000 members from forty-two organizations of Registered Technician
  Engineers.
 Institution of Chemical Engineers.
  Frequency: most years since 1969.
  Coverage: chemical engineers.
  Data source: 800 members of the Institution.
 Institutions of Electrical, Civil, and Mechanical Engineers.
  Frequency: annual.
  Coverage: joint survey of electrical, civil, and mechanical engineers.
  Data source: about 10,000 members in each Institution.
 Institution of Electrical and Electronics Technician Engineers.
  Frequency: annually since 1976.
  Coverage: electrical engineering technicians.
  Data source: 5,800 members.
 Lloyd Executive Selection Incomes Research Unit.
  Frequency: annually, first report in 1975.
  Coverage: professional engineers of all types.

       Data source: 77 engineering companies employing 2,500 engineers.
Technical, Administrative and Supervisory Section of AUEW.
       Frequency: annually. Produced for over fifty years.
       Coverage: members of union.
       Data source: about 75,000 staff in 1,500 establishments.

GEOLOGISTS

Institution of Geologists.
       Frequency: first survey in 1977.
       Coverage: professional geologists.
       Data source: 500 members of the Institution.

GRADUATES

Standing Conference of Employers of Graduates.
       Frequency: annually since 1972.
       Coverage: graduates taking up first appointments.
       Data source: 100 organizations.
Business Graduates Association.
       See under Business Graduates.

INDUSTRIAL ARTISTS

Society of Industrial Artists and Designers.
       Frequency: about every two years. First in 1970.
       Coverage: industrial artists.
       Data source: 600 members of the Society.

INFORMATION SCIENTISTS

Institute of Information Scientists.
       Frequency: full survey five-yearly, annual sample survey.
       Coverage: information scientists.
       Data source: 50 members for annual sample and 1,000 members for full survey.

INSURANCE

Association of Insurance Managers in Industry and Commerce.
       Frequency: biennial.
       Coverage: insurance managers.
       Data source: 200 members of the Association.
Chartered Insurance Institute.
       Frequency: triennial.
       Coverage: professional insurance staff.
       Data source: 4,000 members of the Institute.
Lloyd Executive Incomes Research Unit.
       Frequency: annually. First report in 1968.
       Coverage: all white-collar employees in insurance firms.
       Data source: 80 organizations with 3,600 employees.

LEGAL
Accountancy Personnel Limited.
    See accountants section.
Bar Association for Commerce, Finance, and Industry/Inbucon.
    Frequency: biennial.
    Coverage: lawyers in commerce, finance, and industry.
    Data source: 240 members working in UK.
Chambers and Partners.
    Frequency: annually since 1974.
    Coverage: lawyers and company secretaries in industry and commerce.
    Data source: 230 individuals.

MANAGEMENT
British Institute of Management/Remuneration Economics Ltd.
    Frequency: annual. First report of this series in 1974.
    Coverage: senior management in industry, commerce, and finance.
    Data source: 400 member companies representing 20,000 individuals.
Hay/MSL Limited.
    Frequency: annually since 1962.
    Coverage: higher-paid management, supervisory, professional technical, and
    administrative jobs.
    Data source: 250 companies.
Inbucon/AIC Salary Research Unit.
    Frequency: annual. First report in 1962.
    Coverage: directors, senior and middle managers in industry.
    Data source: 7,000 executives in 580 companies.
Institution of Works Managers.
    Frequency: irregularly.
    Coverage: works managers.
    Data source: 400 members.
Management Centre Europe.
    Frequency: annual. First report in 1965.
    Coverage: senior management in industry, commerce, and finance.
    Data source: 79 companies with 1,700 executive and middle management staff.
Lloyds Executive Incomes Research Unit.
    Frequency: annually. First report in 1975.
    Coverage: senior management in manufacturing and services.
    Data sources: 4,300 managers in 150 companies.

MATHEMATICIANS
Institute of Mathematics and its Applications.
    Frequency: triennial. First report in 1968.
    Coverage: practising mathematicians.
    Data source: 3,700 members of the Institute.

METALLURGISTS
Institute of Metallurgists.
    Frequency: triennial.

Coverage: metallurgists.
Data source: 2,900 members of the Institute.

OFFICE STAFF
Alfred Marks Bureau.
Frequency: quarterly. First report in 1967.
Coverage: clerical and secretarial office staff.
Data source: registrants with the Bureau.
Hay/MSL Limited.
Frequency: twice yearly. First report in 1974.
Coverage: clerical and related office and computer staff.
Data source: 78 companies in London and Bristol.
Institute of Administrative Management.
Frequency: annually. First report in 1942. No survey in 1977.
Coverage: office workers.
Data source: 1,200 organizations with 70,000 individuals.

PHYSICISTS
Institute of Physics.
Frequency: triennial, interim surveys in 1975 and 1976. Initial report in 1948.
Coverage: physicists.
Data source: 5,000 members of the Institute.

PUBLIC RELATIONS
Institute of Public Relations.
Frequency: triennial.
Coverage: public relations personnel.
Data source: 340 members of the Institute.

RESEARCH AND DEVELOPMENT
Reward Regional Surveys Limited.
Frequency: annually. First report 1976.
Coverage: research and development personnel.
Data sources: 2,500 staff in 40 companies.

SALES PERSONNEL
Institution of Sales Management.
Frequency: irregular.
Coverage: salesmen.
Data source: 180 contacts of the Institution.
Institution of Sales Engineers.
Frequency: annual. First report in 1972, discontinued in 1977.
Coverage: sales engineers and sales managers.
Data source: 360 members of the Institution.
Tack Research Ltd.
Frequency: biennial. First report in 1965.
Coverage: about 30,000 salesmen in 600 companies.
Data source: 700 companies.

United Commercial Travellers' Association.
   Frequency: biennial.
   Coverage: salesmen and sales managers.
   Data source: 3,000 members of the Association.

5.4.2. *Reward*

Reward [QRL 66] is another salary survey. It has been excluded from the listing in Section 5.4.1 because we wish to give it special coverage here. This is because it is by far the largest national survey available and has a much more comprehensive coverage than other private surveys.

Reward is a joint publication sponsored by four bodies; the government-financed Professional and Executive Recruitment agency (PER), the Institute of Personnel Management (IPM), the Institute of Directors, and Synergy Publishing Limited. The survey is published by Synergy but *Reward* itself is a partnership which also includes a consultancy service. The information in *Reward* is based on an analysis of the salaries of men and women registering at any of the PER offices. The survey was first published in 1975 and is produced three times each year—March, July, and November. The service was heralded by an explanatory article in the May 1975 *Gazette* [QRL 24], entitled ' "Reward" for employers'. The total cost of the service, which includes the information services of thirty-six Regional Offices and the Central Consultancy Unit, was about £45 in 1977, though members or clients of the managing organizations can obtain it at a reduced rate.

The information provided in *Reward* is based on the present or last salaries of registrants over three four-month periods each year. Since over 100,000 individuals pass through PER each year the sample is large enough for meaningful figures to be produced for these four-month periods. Furthermore, the size of the sample, even though it may be biased because it relies on registrants, is sufficiently large for details on a multiple breakdown by occupation, age, and earnings distribution, and by region to be given. Earnings figures for thirty-five occupations are currently (1978) recorded; these occupations are defined by the CODOT classification of job titles, as given in the *CODOT Directory* [B 37]. The occupations in this classification are well defined so that little ambiguity creeps into this survey, in contrast with the delineation problems which are present in many of the other salary surveys. These occupations range from general management to sales representatives and from accountants to chemists.

The individuals who register at PER are all people seeking a change of job, some of whom will be recently unemployed. This suggests that the individuals considered may not be a representative sample of a parent population which includes all the salary earners in the occupations in question. One might suppose that there is a downward bias to the figures since successful employees are less likely to feature in the register and neither will those who are confident enough to search for jobs through their own endeavours. *Reward* has itself recognized these drawbacks in its sample and recommends in the foreword to each issue the weighting factors which might be applied to scale up the earnings figures to make the sample more representative of the whole population. In 1977 this factor was 1.04, i.e. it was thought that the sample estimates might understate the population figures by about 4 per cent. Other weighting factors are suggested in order to adjust for differences in the sizes of organizations. The basis for these adjustments is, however, rather dubious and it seems most unlikely that these crude corrections can really be applied across the whole age and earnings distributions.

Nevertheless the detail afforded by the surveys and their up-to-dateness cannot be matched by any of the other surveys. Additional information which is given covers the numbers of candidates registered with PER by occupation and region, and the number of vacancies notified on the same basis. In each issue there is also information on regional living costs and salary requirements and special features on topics of interest such as pensions and taxes. A further service which is available, although at a cost of £35, is a special analysis of any other occupation registered at PER but not covered in the survey. Not more than about a third of those registered at PER feature in the thirty-five CODOT groups used in *Reward*. However, the salaries of all sorts of other groups are on file and can be extracted in the same format as used in *Reward* if requested. It is thus possible to obtain earnings information on very small groups of specialists which is available nowhere else. The disadvantage of such data, however, is that the sample size in these cases is so small that the results must be treated with extreme caution. The larger samples, which are published, must also be treated with care, but they provide information which is as good as the better examples of the other smaller surveys listed in Section 5.4.1.

CHAPTER 6

FRINGE BENEFITS AND LABOUR COSTS

6.1. Introduction

So far we have been dealing with cash payments made to persons in return for their labour services. We first examined wage rates and salary scales, the basic minimum entitlements for many workers, and then looked at earnings. But it has long been recognized that there may be many advantages in a job which are not of a pecuniary nature. The covering words for all these different types of non-pecuniary benefits are 'fringe benefits' or 'perks'. The concept of 'total remuneration' has also been introduced, initially in America, to describe the total of pay plus fringe benefits (see Fallick's paper on 'The growth of top salaries in the post-war period' [B 16] for a discussion of this concept). Viewed from the employers' side these various fringe benefits all represent one part of his total labour costs. This is why the two concepts of fringe benefits and labour costs are treated together in the present section.

6.2. Fringe Benefits

The term fringe benefits applies to all of the benefits that a worker receives from his firm apart from the actual payments made to him in his pay-packet. These include subsidized meals, company cars, sports facilities, pension schemes, sick schemes, low interest loans for housing and travel, and all other types of benefit which are not directly reflected in the pay-packet. Of course it is in the nature of these benefits that they are very difficult to quantify. Little information is collected about them and, even when known, it is often very difficult to cost their value to the recipient. For this reason it is sometimes thought more useful to look at an employer's total labour costs in order to gauge how extensive fringe benefits are in any firm or organization. Unfortunately one then has to deal with problems such as the employers' compulsory national insurance contributions. Whilst these are clearly a cost to the employer, they are rarely regarded as a benefit to the employee.

There are no published official sources of statistics on fringe benefits although it is clear that, for tax purposes, the Inland Revenue must have a great deal of unpublished information on some of these benefits. One therefore has to rely on unofficial material, mainly in the form of survey data, from a variety of sources.

One of the earlier studies of fringe benefits in Britain was G. L. Reid and D. J. Robertson's *Fringe Benefits, Labour Costs and Social Security* [QRL 10]. This book, published in 1965, reported the results of a survey of fringe benefits carried out by researchers at Glasgow University. It covered a sample of over three hundred large establishments employing almost three-quarters of a million employees. But the sample was limited to manual workers only, where fringe benefits are generally thought to be less substantial. The importance of nineteen different types of fringe benefit was considered and results were given for different industries as well as for the sample in total. As with most of these surveys its usefulness is limited through its being confined to the one year, but it is nevertheless the most comprehensive of the earlier studies.

A later study by J. Moonman, *The Effectiveness of Fringe Benefits in Industry* [QRL 7], also covered about three-quarters of a million employees, but looked at all workers and not just manuals. The study, published in 1973, was derived from a survey of forty-six companies and isolated eleven different types of fringe benefit. It was rather heavily concentrated on large firms in London and the south-east and may therefore be biased from that point of view. It includes a most useful bibliography of books, pamphlets, and articles on fringe benefits.

The British Institute of Management's *Fringe Benefits for Executives; a Survey of 230 Companies* [QRL 33] was a survey carried out in 1970. A later volume, *Employee Benefits Today* [QRL 29], was published in 1974. The Institute has also published pamphlets on *Management Holidays* [QRL 51], *Luncheon Vouchers* [QRL 50], and *Subsistence and Travelling Expenses in the UK* [QRL 76], all in 1972. The British Institute of Management continues to publish surveys in this field.

An earlier survey, which was available to subscribers only, was the Institute of Personnel Management's *Survey of Fringe Benefits* [QRL 78] conducted in 1966.

There are several other studies which are similarly available only to subscribers. Incomes Data Services regularly devotes issues of its *Income Data Studies* series to topics such as sick-pay, holiday pay, and white-collar allowances [QRL 42]. These special studies are carried out fairly regularly so that there is a certain amount of continuity, although the company coverage tends to change. A full list of these studies is provided in Incomes Data Services' annual index to its reports and studies.

Another private body, Industrial Relations Services, has produced similar reports on topics such as holiday entitlements, house purchase and removal schemes, and sick-pay schemes. These reports are also only available to subscribers (see Section 2.4.1).

Several of the salary surveys already referred to in Section 5.4 also mention some fringe benefits. The Inbucon/AIC Salary Research Unit, for instance, has for many years been conducting surveys of salaries and fringe benefits in Britain and abroad. Generally speaking, the surveys of management or executive pay tend to pay rather more attention to fringe benefits than other surveys although the whole area of fringe benefits is rather under-researched when compared with salaries information.

The Royal Commission on the Distribution of Income and Wealth's report on *Higher Incomes from Employment* [QRL 36] includes a chapter on fringe benefits and superannuation, but this tends to record the results of surveys and research conducted elsewhere. It is nevertheless a useful compendium of existing statistics and provides a good introduction to the subject.

6.3. Labour Costs

The concept of labour costs is wider than that of total remuneration. Whereas all fringe benefits will be a cost to the firm, not all labour costs will appear as a benefit to the employee. The employers' compulsory national insurance contributions have already been mentioned as one example of a cost to the firm that may not be regarded as a benefit by the employee. But there are other, perhaps better, examples. Recruitment costs, for instance, are a charge to the employer but are of no direct benefit to the employee.

6.3.1. *Official labour cost surveys*

Since 1964 the Department of Employment has periodically carried out major surveys of employers' total labour costs. Such surveys took place for 1964 and 1968. A further survey took place for 1973 under the auspices of the EEC and such surveys are now being held every three years (see below). An earlier ILO enquiry, *Labour Costs in Europe* [QRL 45], took place for 1955 on a limited scale and covered only a few industries. That enquiry was part of an International Labour Office enquiry but the 1964 and 1968 enquiries were organized solely by the Department. These enquiries were prompted by the growing recognition that more information was needed about total labour costs and not just wages and salaries, their major constituent part. Commencing in 1952, the European Economic Community carried out surveys of labour costs in industries covered by the Iron and Steel Treaty. Certain manufacturing industries were surveyed in two triennial cycles over the period 1959–64. In 1966 the Community undertook a further survey which, for the first time, covered all manufacturing industries in the same year. The United Kingdom surveys for 1973 and 1975 have been incorporated into the EEC framework. Since 1974 the Department has also been involved in the EEC surveys of labour costs in distribution, insurance, and banking (Section 6.3.2).

The first major survey of labour costs in Great Britain was conducted for 1964. The main results were published in the December 1966 and March 1967 issues of the *Gazette* [QRL 24]. The full results were later published in 1968 in a single booklet produced by the Department entitled *Labour Costs in Great Britain in 1964* [QRL 46].

The 1964 enquiry covered all the industries in the index of production (1958 SIC Orders II to XVIII), part of transport and communications, most of insurance and banking, and the non-industrial civil service and local authorities. In the manufacturing sector the sample used was the register of addresses already used by the Department for its annual enquiry into the earnings of administrative, technical, and clerical workers (Section 5.3.2). All enterprises with 1,000 or more employees were sampled plus 20 per cent of those with 250–999 employees and 10 per cent of those with 25–249 employees. Firms with less than 25 employees were excluded. In non-manufacturing full coverage was obtained in certain areas—for instance, the nationalized industries—where information was available from a central source. In other industries the same sampling procedures as used in manufacturing were employed, with the exception of construction and road passenger transport where, because there are many small firms, 10 per cent of those with 11–24 employees were also sampled.

Seven types of labour costs were isolated by the survey: wages and salaries, statutory national insurance contributions, private social welfare (pensions, sickness, accident, redundancy schemes), payments in kind, subsidized services (canteens, luncheon vouchers, housing, recreational facilities, transport), recruitment and training, and other labour costs. Information on the cost of these various categories was requested for the calendar year 1964, or if more convenient for the financial year ending not later than 5 April 1965. In total, returns were received giving details for just over 8,000,000 employees. The results were presented for different sizes of firm and for different industries, with the expenditure per employee on each type of cost and the percentage of total cost that each category accounted for.

Later surveys, on the same lines as that for 1964, were conducted for 1968 and 1973. The 1968 survey adopted most of the International Labour Office's 'International Standard Classification of Labour Costs' so that there were slight changes from the 1964 survey which were fully explained when the Department published the results in the booklet *Labour Costs in Great Britain in 1968* [B 47]. The main results were also published in the August and October 1970 and January 1971 issues of the *Gazette* [QRL 24]. A parallel enquiry was held for 1968 in Northern Ireland but the results were published separately in the October 1970 *Gazette* [QRL 24]. The additional information obtained for 1968 was the total number of hours worked during the year and details of costs created by three new pieces of legislation, the Industrial Training Act of 1964, the Redundancy Payments Act of 1965, and the Selective Employment Payments Act of 1966. The sampling procedures and coverage of the 1968 enquiry were similar to the 1964 enquiry, but more comprehensive results were published.

The 1973 survey in industry was carried out at the request of the EEC which holds a labour-cost survey every three years and had held one for 1972 (before British membership). The United Kingdom carried out a similar survey for 1975 which brought them into line with the phasing of the EEC survey, and will probably carry out the survey every three years along with the other EEC countries. The 1973 survey, though a year later than the EEC survey, was based on the EEC questionnaire, so that the format differed from the 1964 and 1968 surveys. The changes, however, were not great; the sample-size threshold was raised from firms with 25 employees to those with 50 employees, five firm-size ranges replaced the previous three, and information was now obtained for operatives and administrative, technical and clerical workers separately for all the different items of cost. The results of the survey were published in articles in the September 1975 and October 1975 *Gazettes* [QRL 24] . The results of the 1975 survey were published in the September, November, and December 1977 *Gazettes* [QRL 24] and will also appear in the publications of the Statistical Office of the EEC.

6.3.2. *Labour costs in distribution, insurance, and banking*

As part of a survey in all EEC countries the Department of Employment also conducted a survey of employers' labour costs in wholesale and retail distribution, insurance, and banking in 1974. The results of the 1974 survey for all the member countries are being published by the Statistical Office of the EEC. Meanwhile the results for Great Britain have been published in the June 1976 *Gazette* [QRL 24], pages 596–605. From 1978 these surveys will be synchronized with those in industry (Section 6.3.1).

This EEC survey was the second of its type, though the United Kingdom was not involved in the first survey in 1970. The format of the survey is much the same as the other EEC labour cost surveys described in the previous section and used in this country in 1973. In distribution, questionnaires were sent to all enterprises with more than 50 employees in retail distribution and 100 employees in wholesale distribution and to a sample of those with 10–49 or 99 employees. In insurance and banking much of the information was supplied by the British Insurance Association and the British Bankers' Association. Nine categories of cost were delineated: wages and salaries, statutory national insurance contributions, redundancy provisions, employers' liability insurance, voluntary social welfare, payments in kind, subsidized services to employees, vocational training, and recruitment costs. Wages and salaries paid to apprentices were included under training costs and not as wages and salaries, following EEC practice.

The results for distribution are analysed by the Minimum List Headings of the Standard Industrial Classification when published in the UK and by the European industrial classification (NACE) when published by the EEC. Figures for six separate size ranges are also given and results for male and female full and part-time workers are tabulated. The results for insurance, banking, and other financial institutions are given only in aggregate. The figures are given as the average hourly amounts per employee, apart from one table which gives the average annual amount per employee. A further table gives the composition of the total of employees in the survey by both full-time and part-time workers.

6.3.3. *Wages and total labour costs—international survey*

Each year the Research Department of the Swedish Employers' Confederation (SAF), Stockholm, produces a publication entitled *Wages and Total Labour Costs for Workers—International Survey* [QRL 82]. The first of these volumes appeared in 1963. Subsequent volumes have included a run of about ten years of annual figures for up to fifteen countries, including Great Britain. The information used is based on national sources and statistics collected by the International Labour Office in Geneva. Industries are classified according to the international classification (ISIC).

The definition of total labour costs has altered through the years, generally as wider coverage has become available in the statistics. It is therefore necessary to read the introduction to each survey in order to understand exactly what is being measured. The sources of the statistics for each country are also given in each volume. Care must be taken in using these statistics (and any in similar international compendia) since the figures cannot always be directly compared.

Use has been made of these Swedish statistics by G. F. Ray of the National Institute of Economic and Social Research. He has produced two articles, 'Labour costs and international competitiveness' [QRL 8] and 'Labour costs in OECD countries 1964–75' [QRL 9], in which he has processed the data, looking at earnings and total labour costs separately.

6.3.4. *Labour costs per unit of output*

Since 1968, series of wages and salaries and labour costs per unit of output have been published each month in the *Gazette* [QRL 24] in Table 134. These series were introduced with an article on 'Statistics on output per head and labour costs in the United Kingdom' in the October 1968 *Gazette,* pages 801–6. From 1971 a monthly series of wages and salaries per unit of output in manufacturing industries was calculated and this was introduced by a short note in the April 1971 *Gazette,* page 360.

Wages and salaries per unit of output are constructed from CSO data on wages and salaries and production and from the monthly index of average earnings. The labour costs per unit of output are constructed in a similar way but with a restrictive definition of labour costs. Since the labour costs surveys are only conducted at irregular intervals (see 6.3.1) it is not possible to use the survey data for this series. Thus only those items of labour cost which are readily available are included—namely, wages and salaries, employers' national insurance contributions, contributions to the Redundancy Fund and to superannuation schemes, etc., and, formerly, selective employment tax premiums and refunds. The two series (wage and salaries per unit of output and labour costs per unit of output) naturally tend to move very closely together. The wages and salaries figures used from 1971 in the construction of the manufacturing industries figure for wages and salaries per unit of output have been derived from the monthly index of average earnings. A series of monthly figures for this index for a period of about seven years is given in the Monthly Statistics section of the *Gazette*. The quarterly figures are given in Table 134 for the whole economy, index of production industries, manufacturing, mining and quarrying, metal manufacture, engineering, vehicles, textiles and gas, electricity and water, and a graph following that table regularly shows costs per unit of output for a period of several years.

CHAPTER 7

HISTORICAL DATA

7.1 Introduction

There are numerous series of historical earnings statistics and many different sources for these series. We shall concentrate on the major series and on two main sources—namely, the *Abstract of British Historical Statistics* [QRL 6] by Mitchell and Deane, and the Department of Employment's *British Labour Statistics; Historical Abstract 1886–1968* [QRL 18]. The former was published in 1962, the latter in 1971. Most researchers will find the series that they want and a reference to the original sources in one of these two volumes.

7.2. Abstract of British Historical Statistics [QRL 6]

This volume by B. R. Mitchell with the collaboration of Phyllis Deane is a compendium of a whole variety of economic, industrial, and demographic statistics from early in the nineteenth century to about 1938. The purpose of the volume is summed up in the General Introduction as

'. . . to provide the users of historical statistics with informed access to a wide range of economic data without the labour of identifying sources or of transforming many annual sources into comparable time series. To some extent, of course, this has already been done in the annual volumes of the Statistical Abstract of the United Kingdom, each of which gives statistics for fifteen years at a time. But the official Abstract begins only in 1840; it has varied through time in its coverage; and its successive issues contain many revisions and changes of concept which make the transcription of a long series a laborious process. We have adopted the latest revisions, made the series comparable where possible and identified the breaks wherever these were evident.'

The authors also give a commentary on the series which they reproduce, outlining the problems in interpreting the data.

There is a separate chapter (number XII) which deals with 'Wages and the Standard of Living'. The introduction to this chapter (pages 338–42) summarizes the available statistics. A lot of the information cited is taken from Gilboy's *Wages in Eighteenth Century England* [B 17], Bowley's *Wages and Income since 1860* [QRL 1], and Chapman and Knight's *Wages and Salaries in the United Kingdom 1920–1938* [B 4]. These books are discussed, and other references, including many articles, are mentioned. Many of these sources are also cited and discussed in Deane and Cole's *British Economic Growth 1688–1955* [B 6], a source which is also used in the Mitchell and

Deane volume. The series reproduced in this latter volume are given in Table 4 below. The sources for each of the series, some of which are composite or derived series, are given before each table in Mitchell and Deane [QRL 6], together with careful notes on the exact derivation of each series.

TABLE 4. *Tables given in Mitchell and Deane [QRL 6].*

1. Indices of Average Wages—UK 1790–1938.
2. Indices of Wage Labourers in London and Lancashire—1700–96.
3. Indices of Average Wages in Certain Industries[1]—UK 1770–1938.
4. Indices of Average Incomes of Wage-earners by Industry Groups[2]—UK 1920–38.

Notes.
1. Agriculture, compositors, building, shipbuilding and engineering, cotton workers, coal-mining, plus (from 1920) iron and steel, woollen and worsted, printing and bookbinding, furniture, gas supply, and railway service.
2. Nineteen industrial groups.

Besides these tables the Mitchell and Deane chapter on Wages and the Standard of Living gives a full list of references at the end of the chapter (pages 359–62) listing a wide range of the books, government publications, and articles on this subject covering the historical period up to the Second World War. Altogether over a hundred references are cited, making the book one of the best first sources to consult for information of historical wage and earnings statistics.

7.3 British Labour Statistics; Historical Abstract 1886–1968 [QRL 18]

As the title implies, this official Department of Employment volume covers a later period than Mitchell and Deane, although there is a substantial overlap of information for the period from the middle of the nineteenth century up to the 1920s. Previously the Department of Employment (though under various different names) had published the *Abstract of Labour Statistics* at irregular intervals—there were twenty-two issues between 1894 and 1937. Then from 1962 to 1968 the Department published a quarterly Bulletin, *Statistics on Incomes, Prices, Employment and Production* [QRL 75]. This contained information collected by other government departments such as the Board of Trade and the Central Statistical Office, but most of the data were provided by the then Ministry of Labour. The advantage of this Bulletin (and the previous Abstract) over the *Gazette* [QRL 24] was that a run of figures for up to ten years was given, whereas the *Gazette* has concentrated on the most recent one or two years. But as from 1969 the quarterly Bulletin was replaced by the annual *British Labour Statistics Yearbooks* [QRL 19], which bring together in a single volume all the main statistics relating to a particular calendar year and some past data, and these were preceded by the *Historical Abstract* [QRL 18] which covers all the statistics up to and including 1968.

The starting date of 1886 in the title of the *Historical Abstract* is not a rigid one, the earliest data being for 1780. But 1886 was the year when the House of Commons passed the motion that '. . . steps should be taken to ensure . . . the full and accurate collection and publication of labour statistics'. The Board of Trade was made responsible for this task and in 1893 established a Labour Department. From May 1893 labour statistics were published in a monthly *Labour Gazette*. The *Gazette* [QRL 24] has been published regularly ever since although it has undergone several changes of name since then, as firstly, it was transferred to the new Ministry of Labour in January 1917, and then, as the name of that Ministry changed. The successive titles have been: the *Labour Gazette* (May 1893–January 1905), the *Board of Trade Labour Gazette* (February 1905–June 1917), the *Labour Gazette* (July 1917–May 1922), the *Ministry of Labour Gazette* (June 1922–May 1968), the *Employment and Productivity Gazette* (June 1968–December 1970) and the *Department of Employment Gazette* (January 1971 onwards). The *Gazette,* under whichever name, is still the best first-hand source of information on official wage and earnings statistics, but the *Historical Abstract* remains one of the best sources for long series. Furthermore, several of the series reproduced in the *Historical Abstract* date from before 1886. Thus several of the tables on wage rates contain statistics dating back to much earlier in the nineteenth century. Most of these figures are from published sources and are available elsewhere, but some are taken from working documents and from unpublished reports by G. H. Wood who worked in the Labour Department of the Board of Trade. His unpublished collection of historical wage rates can be found in the library of the Royal Statistical Society, but much of his work is available in the *Historical Abstract* [QRL 18].

The earliest entry in the *Historical Abstract* is for wages in the printing industry in 1780 [QRL 18, Table 4]. But, as can be seen from the List of Tables reproduced here in Appendix F, several of the series start in the first half of the nineteenth century and are taken up to 1968 by various linking devices. Data are given on both wage rates and earnings. Some of the series are given as rates of pay in shillings and (old) pence whilst others are given in index form. Up to the Second World War the occupations covered are rather mixed and there are gaps in the data for many of the series. But for the period 1947 to 1968 the coverage of wage rates is excellent with the actual values of basic weekly wage rates for men in about one hundred and fifty occupations covered by collective agreements and statutory orders being given (Table 10). Indices of basic weekly wage rates for all manual workers in the United Kingdom are given for each month from June 1934 to December 1968 and for each June and December in the period 1920 to 1933 (Table 13). A breakdown of this index for men, women, and juveniles separately is given for each month from June 1947 to December 1968 (Table 15) and the same period is also covered for all workers, by eighteen industry groups (Tables 18 and 19). These are the major tables; the contents of the other tables can be seen in the listing shown in Appendix F. Figures since 1968 can usually be found quite easily in the *British Labour Statistics Yearbooks* [QRL 19].

In addition to the statistics on wage rates, the *Historical Abstract* reproduces the main results of all the earnings surveys from 1886 to 1968 inclusive, including an analysis of the dispersion of earnings over this period, and the pioneering results of the first *New Earnings Survey* in 1968. It gives the monthly index of average earnings from 1963 onwards and analyses of hours of work, holiday entitlements, and comparisons between earnings and wage rates (from 1935 onwards).

7.4. Other Sources of Historical Statistics on Earnings

So far we have reviewed the two major secondary sources of statistics on earnings of an historical nature. Those two volumes serve as an excellent introduction to the statistics which are available, and are also a good starting-point for references to further collections of statistics and to the original sources. In this section we briefly mention a few other major reference books which also discuss much of this information and are readily available from libraries.

There are two comparative international studies of pay structures in the United Kingdom and other countries. Reynolds and Taft's *The Evolution of Wage Structure* [B 32] looks at pay in France, Sweden, Great Britain, Canada, and the United States for the inter-war and immediate post-war periods. This study looks in particular at changing occupational differentials, using information from a variety of studies which are cited. There is a separate chapter on the position in Britain (pages 251–85) as well as comparisons between Britain and the other countries. A similar comparison is made in Phelps Brown and Browne's *A Century of Pay* [B 31] which examines the course of pay and production in France, Germany, Sweden, the United Kingdom, and the United States over the period 1860–1960. The countries are not dealt with separately since the approach is chronological but there is a useful list of sources for the United Kingdom statistics in Appendix 2, pages 398–418.

A book which is devoted solely to the situation in this country is Routh's *Occupation and Pay in Great Britain 1906–1960* [B 33]. This book introduces a whole variety of wage and earnings statistics, examining as far as possible differences over time in the pay of different occupations and skills. For most of the groups concerned Routh has managed to obtain figures relating to the pre-First World War period, the inter-war period, and the post-war period. The majority of the data cited are for salaries or earnings but wage rates have frequently been used when earnings figures have not been available. A slightly more theoretical book, which tries to explain differences in earnings, is Lydall's *The Structure of Earnings* [B 27], published in 1968.

At one time no official wage rates index was published, despite the fact that information on wage rates was regularly collected and published. Unofficial wage rates indices were therefore constructed by private researchers. Thus in the inter-war period Professor A. L. Bowley (whose work has already been cited) compiled an index which was based on 1924 and used the 1924 wage bill for weighting purposes. This index was regularly published in the *London and Cambridge Economic Service Bulletin* [QRL 49] and is also described in Bowley's *Wages and Income in the United Kingdom since 1860* [QRL 1], but it was superseded after the war by the official index which had been developed by the Director of Statistics at the Ministry of Labour, E. C. Ramsbottom, who had himself been producing an index by industry group in the 1930s.

A similar situation developed in the post-war period, by which time an official index was being produced, but no indices for different industries were being published. This led Devons to complain in his *British Economic Statistics* [B 7], that the official industrial figures which were produced for the International Labour Office *Yearbook of Labour Statistics* [QRL 84], were not being published in this country. Until March 1954 figures for a limited range of occupations in individual industries were given by Bowley in the *London and Cambridge Economic Service Bulletin* [QRL 49], but from then there was a gap of four years before an alternative series was produced.

A new series of wage rate indices by SIC Order was produced in 1958 by Devons and Ogley. Their indices went back to 1948, which they used as their base date, and their weights were determined by the 1948 wage bill. The information on wage rates which they used was taken from the official sources; namely, the annual *Time Rates of Wages and Hours of Work* [QRL 81] and the monthly table on principal changes in the *Gazette* [QRL 24].

This *index* was published in successive issues of the Manchester School in 1959 and 1960 by Crossley [QRL 2], but had soon started to be published in the *Guardian* newspaper and in the newly started *National Institute Economic Review* [QRL 54]. A complete run of these wage indices was published in (1964) in Devons and Crossley's *The Guardian Wage Indexes* [QRL 4]. Separate wage rates indices for men and for women are given for twenty-three of the twenty-four SIC Orders (Order XXI of the 1948 SIC, Insurance, Banking, and Finance, being excluded) for each year from 1949 to 1960, and for each month in 1961. Both weekly and hourly rates are given and for the weekly rates the individual agreements are listed. For comparative purposes the official statistics on average earnings by industry from the biannual enquiry are also tabulated but these do not cover SIC Orders II, XX, XXI, XXIII, and XXIV, which are mining and quarrying and some services (see Section 4.4 for details of this enquiry).

The Devons Wage Indices were produced up to the end of 1965. Full runs of annual figures of weekly wage rates for men and women were published in a final article 'Wage Rate Indexes by Industry, 1948–1965' by Devons, Crossley, and Maunder [QRL 5], published in 1968. By then an official index was being published giving details by main order, although not by sex and agreement (this was the 1956 based series). Much work would also have been necessary in re-basing and re-weighting so the compilers decided to discontinue their series. For the benefit of future researchers they provided a comparison of movements in the Devons series and the then Ministry of Labour series for the period 1956–65. They found that there was a slightly greater rise in their index than in the official index, but the difference for the components was by no means consistent. They concluded that '. . . on the whole it would appear that . . . the level of agreement is quite satisfactory' [QRL 5, page 396]. This conclusion was not entirely unexpected since the two indices were both based on the official information on nationally agreed rates. Although the Devons index is readily available for the period 1948–65, most researchers now tend to use the official index which is available for a longer period and with good industrial coverage in the *Historical Abstract* [QRL 18].

A volume which collected together information on wage rates in the period 1851–1906 was published by the Labour Department of the Board of Trade in 1908. This was titled *Rates of Wages and Hours of Labour in Various Industries in the UK, 1851–1906* [QRL 57] and covered building, coal, iron, engineering, shipbuilding, other metal trades, textiles, clothing, printing, and woodworking. It was produced for internal use in the Department and therefore few copies exist.

A summary of the existing official wage rates data was provided in 1958 in an article, 'Official Indices of Rates of Wages, 1880–1957', published in the *Gazette* [QRL 24] of April 1958 (pages 132–5). Although this provides a good introduction to the official data for that period, it has also been superseded by the *Historical Abstract* [QRL 18] which remains the best initial source for the historical statistics on both wage rates and earnings.

CHAPTER 8

EVALUATION

It is clear from the preceding chapters that there is no scarcity of data on earnings. But the questions we turn to in this concluding section are how useful and how adequate these data are for the purposes of negotiators, policy makers, and researchers. The needs of these different groups of users are fairly widely spread, so that it is not easy to give a simple answer. Furthermore, it is often the case that the user of statistics is insufficiently aware of the nature and method of collection or compilation of the figures which he is using. This lack of knowledge of the data being used, which is either the fault of the user due to inadequate background research, or, perhaps less frequently, the fault of the presenter of the statistics in not properly qualifying them, commonly results in the data being misinterpreted and therefore misused. It is of course one of the purposes of reviews such as the present one to try to make clearer the nature of the statistics which are available, but a general caveat to users, to check the sources, and to presenters, to underline the limitations of particular series, is probably worth repeating. A further object of this concluding section is therefore to point out some of the more important pitfalls in the use of the statistics on earnings which have been reviewed. But it is also important to know the limitations of the data, so we start by looking at the coverage of statistics in this field in order to point out any gaps that exist.

8.1. Coverage

8.1.1. *Wage rates*

We have already mentioned (Section 2.1) that the official material on wage rates is confined to nationally negotiated collective agreements and Wages Boards and Councils. The reporting of the details of these in the *Gazette* [QRL 24] and the two other main sources [QRL 21 and 81] is very good. However, one cannot over emphasize the fact that the wage rates so reported are minimum entitlements and relate only to national agreements. Company or plant agreements, which are important in many industries, particularly the engineering industry, are not reported by the Department of Employment. Information on such agreements is by its nature difficult to obtain, but with the exception of certain periods of incomes policies, the systematic monitoring of these agreements has not been regarded as a function of the Department. Official statistics have therefore concentrated on national rates and average earnings.

If one wishes to obtain information on the rates of pay negotiated in company or plant agreements one must look at a variety of private sources (see Section 2.4). These private sources provide much information on such agreements but it appears that the combination of official and unofficial reporting of wage rates still does not provide a comprehensive picture for the whole economy. In this area there is undoubtedly a gap in the information which is readily available. It may be impossible to fill this gap given that, first, there is no requirement to report or make public agreements reached under collective bargaining arrangements and, secondly, the rates of pay for many jobs are not covered by such agreements. Nevertheless the danger is that the very extensive coverage of national rates provided in official sources will, *faute de mieux,* be taken as representative of the totality of wage rates in the economy. It is therefore necessary to proceed with caution and care when using official wage rates information, whilst recognizing that it may nevertheless be the most reliable and long-established source of wage rates information that is available.

The drawbacks arising from the emphasis on national rates in the official reporting of wage rates of course extend to the wage rates index (Section 2.3). This is regarded by some users as being an early indicator of the current level of wage settlements. It is certainly up to date, the latest monthly figures being released within three weeks of the month in question. But it is open to question whether it is really a good indicator of the 'going' level of settlement. This matter is discussed in some detail in Elliott and Dean [B 13]. If one twelfth of all workers settled each month then the index might approximate to a measure of the 'average settlement', but since the sequence of settlements is far from being so uniform either through the year or from year to year, the index cannot give a clear indication of the average level of the latest settlements. The official line is that this is not what the index purports to do, but the problem is that this is how some users interpret it. Ironically, however, the index may serve this purpose in a different way. When the index moves in an irregular fashion this may alert the user to an abnormal movement in one of its constituent settlements. This happened in a major way in 1978 when the introduction of a new national engineering agreement, after a gap of more than two years, led to a sudden surge in the index (see May 1978 *Gazette*). To assess the importance of a movement in the index one must therefore look at the settlements which take effect during the month—the increases achieved and the numbers involved. But this only emphasizes the limitations of the index. It might be more sensible, therefore, to consider the possibility of having a series which does attempt to measure the average level of settlements in the most recent past, in contrast with the official index which only measures changes in the average level of nationally negotiated wage rates. Such a series has been constructed at Aberdeen University by Elliott and Shelton [B 14]; but even such a settlements series, being based on national agreements, would fail to reflect the movements in rates at the shop-floor level. It is in that area that the main gaps exist in the information on wages.

8.1.2. *Earnings*

In passing from the examination of wage rates to that of earnings we pass from a fairly narrow concept of pay—the standard rates paid to manual workers—to a fairly broad concept (the definition of earnings is discussed in Section 4.1). This gives rise to one of the difficulties involved in using earnings data, for the definition or coverage of earnings varies between the many official and unofficial sources in this area. The user must therefore take care to find out exactly what each earnings series describes in order to avoid misinterpretation. Furthermore most of the data on earnings are given in the form of averages or medians for a whole group of persons and this means that such data must be treated most carefully if comparisons across groups or through time are going to be made. A difference in absolute values for average earnings between two groups, for instance, may reflect no difference in pay for two individuals with similar work characteristics, but may be due solely to the varying skill, sex, or age composition of the two work-forces being considered. Absolute levels of earnings must therefore be interpreted with caution; movements in absolute levels between points in time may prove more reliable. However, even movements must be treated with care unless it is known that the sample has remained fairly stable through time.

The variety of the information on average earnings is immense. But its usefulness depends to a large extent on the continuity of the series in question and on the manner in which the information is collected and presented. The *New Earnings Survey* [QRL 55] has answered many of the criticisms of gaps in the official earnings statistics that were voiced in the 1950s and 1960s. But one limitation of the survey is that in considering trends over a period of years one must remember that it has only had a continuous annual existence in its present form since 1970. Since 1970, however, it has provided by far the richest source of information on earnings that is available in this or any other country. Many features of the survey are major innovations, in particular the publication of results for 'matched' samples of workers from year to year.

At the risk of seeming over critical of what is in most respects an excellent source of earnings data, one should perhaps mention a few of the minor drawbacks of the NES. First, it is based on PAYE records and therefore 'misses' quite a number of part-time workers who are below the tax threshold, some workers who are in the process of changing jobs in the period early in the year when the addresses of the relevant employers are extracted from the tax records, and any tax-avoiders (though the latter are covered in no statistics). Secondly, it does refer to one pay week or pay period so that it is not possible to calculate an annual total for earnings from the NES figures. A third handicap with the NES is that the earnings information that it provides at any one time may well be fairly dated. There is an inevitable delay of some months before publication as employers return forms and as the information is checked and processed, so that the six-month publication lag that presently exists is in many ways commendably short. But since the NES is carried out only once a year there is a maximum 'most recent information' lag of up to eighteen months, which means that the usefulness of the NES for some immediate policy purposes is lost. Lastly, there are inevitably some small reservations with some of the questions asked and the way the material is presented. For instance, the make-up of pay question, which provides invaluable information, gives a figure for 'all other pay' which is mostly composed of 'basic pay', but it does not answer the question of what proportion of pay is accounted for by nationally negotiated rates. Arguably it may be very difficult to get answers to such a question in a national survey which covers many people who are not on national agreements at all and many others whose employers do not know what the national agreement says. Nevertheless, the absence of such information makes it very difficult to link these average earnings figures with the official wage rates figures in any meaningful way. Some help in linking wage rates and earnings might be achieved if there were an analysis of the make-up of pay by occupation and agreement. Such an analysis should be possible using existing NES data but would involve a lot of processing.

The attempt to link figures for earnings and wage rates, made in Table 125 in the

Gazette [QRL 24], which compares the OES figures of manual workers' earnings with the wage rates index, might be considered misleading. A problem in comparing these two series is that the wage rates index is a fixed weight series whilst the average earnings series is effectively current weighted (see Section 4.4). This table, which until September 1970 was actually titled 'Wage drift', may be misinterpreted unless used very carefully and it is therefore unfortunate that greater qualification is not given in the footnotes to the table.

The monthly index of average earnings (Section 4.2), being published within two months of the month in question, provides a more rapid indicator of movements in average earnings than does the NES. On this count alone it is thus a most useful series. But the rapidity of its production entails costs, the main one being that the analysis it gives is rather limited. It provides information on the average earnings of all employees, and results are given for the main industrial groups. Also, the figures for all manufacturing industries, and all industries and services covered by the 'old' index, are seasonally adjusted. The 'older' index does not have a particularly comprehensive coverage, although the publication of a broader index since 1976 has remedied this shortcoming (see Section 4.2.4). But separate figures for males and females are not given, nor is there any indication of the amount of overtime or other payments each month. This may be regarded as unfair criticism since the monthly index is deliberately based on a simple form in order to ensure the maximum returns from employers without delay. Nevertheless there is clearly a gap in the official earnings information between the two-month-old monthly index and the six to eighteen-month-old NES, although it might be one that is costly to fill.

This particular gap is not adequately filled by the October earnings survey or by the other official sources which have been described in Section 5. The OES (see Section 4.4) fills in part of the year's gap in NES information but refers only to manual workers.

The other official sources (Section 5) each have their uses but also fail to be either comprehensive or to be on comparable bases to the main sources. Neither is this gap between the monthly index and NES filled by unofficial sources. Such sources also tend to cover just small areas of the economy (this is especially true of the salary surveys) and also rely on a wide variety of collection methods. Generally speaking, there is little continuity in any of the unofficial sources and their reliability is open to question. However, this is not to deny the usefulness of some of the unofficial sources. Incomes Data Services, for instance, in both their *Reports* [QRL 41] and *Studies* [QRL 42], provide an extremely useful commentary on the labour market as well as a fairly good coverage of the latest settlements and valuable in-depth studies of particular industries or groups of workers.

8.1.3. *Other material*

The material on salary scales, which one might expect would complement the wage rates statistics, does not do this at all. There is little information on salary scales, although the NALGO source (Section 3.2.1) is by far the best in this field, but a confusing amount on the average earnings of salaried workers. The official index of salaries (Section 5.3.3) is of this form, and being based on NES information, is rather out of date so far as any current negotiations are concerned. Recent information on new salary scales is sometimes reported by Incomes Data Services but this coverage is not extensive and is rather haphazard. The drawbacks of the multitude of salary surveys have already been mentioned in Section 5.4.1 whilst the reports of the Review Bodies, Royal Commissions, and committees of enquiry (Section 3.3) tend to be *ad hoc*. Despite the amount of statistics on salaries one must therefore conclude that apart from the NES there are no good reliable sources in this field.

When we move to the broader concept of total remuneration (Chapter 6) we find that there is a similar lack of comprehensiveness in the available statistics. Fringe benefits are a largely under-researched field whilst statistics on labour costs have in the past been collected in a rather irregular fashion. Once again, given the difficulties in obtaining data in this area in the first place, it is perhaps not surprising that there is a gap in the coverage, but it is surely one of the areas of wages and earnings statistics where improvement should be possible.

8.2. Reliability of the Data

We have already mentioned that many of the unofficial sources of statistics are not particularly reliable. This is a fairly broad brush with which to criticize the unofficial sources but in general it is true. In particular cases the statistics are both reliable and useful. In most cases it is possible to judge the reliability of the data by looking at the methods of collection and in particular the sampling techniques. One must take special care with any sources where the degree of self-assessment is high. Whenever there is any great dependence of data recorded on observer judgement, a sense of caution is advisable.

With one notable exception—namely, the NES—there is very little discussion of the reliability of statistics in the descriptions of the published results. In the NES results are generally not given unless there are one hundred or more persons in the sample for the category concerned and unless the standard error of the estimate of average gross weekly earnings is 2.0 per cent or less. Furthermore, in the main tables of earnings by occupation, industry, and agreement, the standard error as a percentage of the estimate is given, where possible, so that the user is able to judge the reliability of the statistics. Such procedures are very welcome but are not possible or do not occur with any of the other sources surveyed.

One persistent problem with nearly all economic statistics, particularly those with short publication lags or with seasonal adjustments, is the tendency for later revisions. This is especially true of the official monthly indices of wage rates and seasonally adjusted average earnings although, given the need for rapid publication, such revisions are scarcely avoidable. Revisions to the index of basic weekly wage rates may be as much as 1 per cent of the total; they are invariably in an upwards direction, usually because of backdating of settlements and occasionally because of delayed reporting. Revisions to the monthly index of average earnings are rarely as much as even a quarter of a per cent of the unadjusted series and are even on occasion in a downward direction. The seasonally adjusted series naturally tends to be revised rather more as extra years are used in the adjustment procedures, but the results are not affected in any major way.

Those series with longer publication lags, such as the NES and October Earnings Enquiry, tend not to be revised at all unless for purposes of correction. However, with the NES there is a tendency for some groups whose normal settlement date is at the beginning of April to 'miss' getting into the April results for the year in question because of backdating of settlements. A good example of this occurred with the April 1975 NES which could not take account of a settlement for civil servants which was made after the date of the NES survey but was backdated to include April. This omission was un-avoidable given the NES procedures at that time but it would have been helpful if it had been footnoted. This particular case was specifically mentioned in the April 1976 NES (page A48) but it is not clear whether action has been taken to prevent a recurrence. The case of the civil servants was anyway a glaring case of 'missing' a settlement but one wonders how often such settlements go unnoticed and are therefore left out of the NES or OES results. It is clearly a case for a further question to the employer along the lines of: '. . . is this worker likely to receive a backdated settlement which will affect his April earnings?' Since the timing of any earnings survey can be quite critical more thought should be given to dealing with those settlements which may 'escape the net' and users of the surveys should also be aware of the possibility of such 'escapes' happening.

Revisions to unofficial sources of statistics in this field are negligible. Late reporting is often not a factor involved in the procedures used and most of the private bodies concerned are not interested in revisions. Matters have improved somewhat since 1978 because where settlements are known to have been delayed or backdated, such information is footnoted.

8.3. Summary and conclusions

Over all the unofficial sources of statistics on earnings are far less reliable than the official sources. But statistics from both sources need to be treated with great care if they are not to be misused.

The long lags in publication mean that much of the information on wages and earnings has little immediate policy value and is too out of date for use by negotiators. The exceptions, the official indices of wage rates and average earnings, are much used by negotiators and policy makers but the danger is that, *faute de mieux,* too much emphasis may be placed on these two sources.

The major drawback of the wage rates index is that it relates only to minimum rates in national agreements. This is a major handicap since much collective bargaining is decentralized. Furthermore, the index is occasionally used as if it was an indicator of average settlements; it is not.

The monthly index of average earnings provides an extremely good and rapid indicator of movements in earnings. But it lacks the detail that is provided by other surveys such as the NES.

The New Earnings Survey is a very rich source of data on earnings but suffers from being conducted only once a year (although the form-fillers probably consider this interval as too short). The nature of the survey may make this inevitable but it unfortunately results in a lag of detailed information on earnings which can be as long as eighteen months.

As far as the other official sources are concerned, if anything one might complain that there are too many of them. It might be better for the official bodies to concentrate on doing two or three surveys extremely well rather than spread their resources over a wide field. It is clear that we require not only the main statistics on wages and earnings provided by the Department of Employment but also a comprehensive monitoring system for all developments in the wages and earnings field. The two important gaps in the statistics which have been mentioned here are comprehensive information on salary scales and details of local company and plant wage agreements. At present one is forced to use a combination of a whole variety of official and unofficial sources, including press cuttings, union contacts, etc., to assess the latest developments in the wages and earnings field.

Furthermore, researchers and others who wish to find a long series of figures from official sources must combine the use of the *British Labour Statistics; Historical Abstract* [QRL 18] with successive *Yearbooks* [QRL 19] and *Gazettes* [QRL 24]. There is clearly a good case for producing a follow-up volume to the *Historical Abstract*, possibly an edition covering the next ten years 1969–78.

It would also be useful for there to be a commentary in the *Gazette* [QRL 24] on the latest developments in the wages and earnings field, covering both official and unofficial sources of information. Statistics tend too often to be too baldly stated. There are strong grounds for thinking that qualifications and commentary on the statistics, when necessary, may reduce the chance of misuse.

The Department of Employment has nevertheless made great efforts in recent years to improve the description, the coverage and the comprehensiveness of its statistics, and has been willing to elaborate upon or qualify its published results more readily (as with the increasing use of footnotes in the NES and with special notes or articles in the *Gazette*). The introduction of the New Earnings Survey, which is now almost ten years old, was a major development and has provided a wealth of material on earnings, much of which has still to be fully exploited by researchers. The extension of the monthly index of average earnings to the whole economy, in 1976, was also a most welcome development. So whilst there are still large gaps in the information available, and it is possible to point out many weaknesses in present procedures, great improvements are being made.

QUICK REFERENCE LIST—TABLE OF CONTENTS

QUICK REFERENCE LIST

Type of data	Breakdown	Area	Frequency	Publication	Text reference
WAGE RATES					
(a) *Individual agreements*	National collective agreements and Wages Councils	UK	Reported monthly	[QRL 21] [QRL 24]	2.2 2.2
	National collective agreements and Wages Councils	UK	Reported annually	[QRL 19] [QRL 81]	2.2
	Same plus company agreements	UK	Reported fortnightly	[QRL 41]	2.4.1
(b) *Official index*					
Basic weekly and basic hourly wage rates; all manual workers	All industries and services; unadjusted and seasonally adjusted. Manufacturing; unadjusted and seasonally adjusted. 18 industry groups; unadjusted	UK	Monthly	[QRL 24]	2.3
Basic weekly wage rates; all manual workers	All industries and services; unadjusted. Manufacturing; unadjusted	UK	Quarterly	[QRL 27]	2.3
Basic weekly wage rates; all manual workers	All industries and services; unadjusted. Manufacturing; unadjusted. 18 industry groups; unadjusted	UK	Monthly	[QRL 52]	2.3
Basic hourly wage rates; all manual workers	All industries and services; unadjusted. Manufacturing; unadjusted	UK	Monthly	[QRL 52]	2.3
Basic weekly and basic hourly wage rates; all manual workers	18 industry groups; unadjusted	UK	Monthly	[QRL 19]	2.3
(c) *Changes in wage rates*	Basic weekly rates of wages in 18 industry groups	UK	Monthly	[QRL 19] [QRL 24] [QRL 52]	2.2
(d) *Historical statistics* Weekly wage rates	Engineering 1851–1968	London Manchester Liverpool Birmingham	Selected years	[QRL 18]	7.3

Weekly wage rates	Building 1810–1968	Sheffield Glasgow Cardiff Belfast London Manchester Liverpool Birmingham Newcastle Leeds Glasgow	Selected years	[QRL 18]	7.3
Weekly wage rates	Printing 1780–1968	Same, plus Hull Aberdeen Dundee Edinburgh Cardiff Belfast	Selected years	[QRL 18]	7.3
Weekly wage rates	Furniture 1810–1968	London Manchester Liverpool Birmingham Newcastle Halifax Preston Leeds Glasgow	Selected years	[QRL 18]	7.3
Weekly wage rates	Footwear 1810–1968	London Northampton Newcastle Kettering Leeds Leicester Bristol Glasgow	Selected years	[QRL 18]	7.3
Weekly wage rates	Agriculture 1850–1968	UK	Annual	[QRL 18]	7.3
Weekly wage rates	44 occupations in 14 industries, 1914–38	UK	Annual	[QRL 18]	7.3
Basic weekly wage rates	Rates for male manual workers in 180 occupations; 1947–68	UK	Annual	[QRL 18]	7.3

WAGE RATES (cont.)
(d) *Historical statistics (cont.)*

Type of data	Breakdown	Area	Frequency	Publication	Text reference
Indices of money and real wages	Labourers, 1700–96	London Lancashire	Annual	[QRL 6]	7.2
Index of average money wages	Manual workers, 1790–1938	GB Ireland	Every 5 years	[QRL 6]	7.2
Index of average money and real wages	Manual workers, 1850–1902	UK	Annual	[QRL 6]	7.2
Index of weekly wage rates	Selection of representative industries, 1874–1936	UK	Annual	[QRL 18]	7.3
Index of money wages	Manual workers, 1880–1936	UK	Annual	[QRL 1]	7.2
Index of basic weekly wage rates	All manual workers, all industries, 1920–68	UK	Monthly	[QRL 18]	7.3
Indices of basic weekly wage rates	Manual workers, men, women, juveniles, and all workers; all industries and all manufacturing industries, 1947–68	UK	Monthly	[QRL 18]	7.3
Indices of basic weekly wage rates	All manual workers, by 18 industries; 1947–68	UK	Monthly	[QRL 18]	7.3
Indices of basic weekly wage rates	Manual workers; men, in 100 industries; 1949–60	UK	Annual	[QRL 4]	7.4
Indices of basic weekly wage rates	Manual workers; women, in 70 industries	UK	Annual	[QRL 4]	7.4
Indices of basic hourly wages rates	All manual workers, all industries; 1920–68	UK	Monthly	[QRL 18]	7.3
Indices of basic hourly wage rates	Manual workers; men, women, juveniles, and all workers; all industries and manufacturing industries; 1947–68	UK	Monthly	[QRL 18]	7.3
Indices of basic hourly wage rates	All manual workers, by 18 industries; 1947–68	UK	Monthly	[QRL 18]	7.3
Indices of basic hourly wage rates	Manual workers; men, and women in 22 industrial groups (main SIC Orders); 1949–60	UK	Annual	[QRL 4]	7.4

SALARY SCALES

Salary scales	List of scales in 32 organizations; 1946 onwards depending on group	UK	Various	[QRL 38]	3.2.1
Salary scales	Various groups reported as new settlements made	UK	Various	[QRL 41] [QRL 42]	3.2.2
Salary scales	Teachers in schools	UK	Annual	[QRL 69]	3.3.2
Salary scales	Teachers in establishments of higher education	UK	Annual	[QRL 68]	3.3.2
Salary scales	Civil servants and Ministers of the Crown	UK	Annual	[QRL 16] [QRL 23]	3.3.4

EARNINGS

(a) *Earnings of manual workers*

Average weekly earnings (October)	Most industries (MLH and SIC Order number), five groups (men over 21, youths and boys under 21, full-time and part-time women over 18, and girls)	UK	Annual	[QRL 19] February issues of [QRL 24]	4.4
Average hourly earnings (October)	Same as above	UK	Annual	February issues of [QRL 24]	4.4
Average weekly and hourly earnings (October)	By standard region and 23 industries for men over 21 and women over 18.	Regions	Annual	[QRL 19] February issues of [QRL 24]	4.4
Average weekly earnings (October)	19 industry groups; men over 21 and women over 18	UK	Annual	[QRL 52]	4.4
Averages, medians and distributions of weekly and hourly earnings (April)	All industries; by sex, by agreement, by industry, by occupation, and by region; various cross classifications	GB and regions	Annual	[QRL 55]	4.3
Average weekly earnings and distributions	Full-time adult men and women; all industries	UK	Annual	[QRL 13]	4.3
Average weekly and hourly earnings (January and June)	By occupation in certain parts of shipbuilding, chemical manufacture, and engineering (June only)	UK	Biannual	May and October issues of [QRL 24] (and [QRL 19] in less detail)	5.2.1

Type of data	Breakdown	Area	Frequency	Publication	Text reference
EARNINGS (cont.)					
(a) Earnings of manual workers (cont.)					
Average weekly and hourly earnings (April)	Certain manufacturing industries (MLH numbers 213, 261, 272, 362, 383, 395, 415, 429, and 431) and service industries (MLH 893 and 895): men (21 and over), youths and boys, full-time women, part-time women, and girls.	UK	Annual	August issues of [QRL 24]	5.2.2
Average weekly earnings (October)	Coal miners	UK	Annual	February issues of [QRL 24], [QRL 13], and [QRL 19]	5.2.3
Average weekly earnings (April and October)	British Rail	UK	Biannual	Various issues of [QRL 24], [QRL.13], and [QRL 19]	5.2.3
Average weekly earnings (April and October)	London Transport	London	Biannual	Various issues of [QRL 24], [QRL 13], and [QRL 19]	5.2.3
Average weekly earnings (October)	Agriculture	GB	Annual	February issues of [QRL 24], [QRL 13], and [QRL 19]	5.2.3
Average weekly earnings	Agriculture. All hired men, youths, women, and girls; 7 occupational categories of male workers; value of payments-in-kind	GB	Quarterly	October issues of [QRL 24]	5.2.4
Average weekly earnings	Agriculture	GB	Annual	[QRL 13]	5.2.4
(b) Earnings of non-manual workers					
Averages, medians and distributions of weekly and hourly earnings (April)	All industries; by sex, by agreement, by industry, by occupation, and by region; various cross-classifications	GB and regions	Annual	[QRL 55]	4.3

Average weekly earnings and distributions (April)	Full-time adult men and women, all industries	UK	Annual	[QRL 13]	4.3
Average weekly earnings (October)	Full-time employees in production industries and in 20 industry groups; males and females	UK	Annual	[QRL 24]	5.3.4
Index of salaries	All non-manual employees (as covered by NES); industries and all manufacturing industries; all ages and full-time adults; men and women separately and together.	GB	Annual	[QRL 24]	5.3.3
Salary surveys	Various groups of non-manual workers	UK and regions	Various	See [QRL 39] and lists in Section 5.4	5.4

(c) Earnings of all workers

Averages, medians and distributions of weekly and hourly earnings of all workers (April)	By age, sex, region, all industries and all manufacturing industries	GB and regions	Annual	[QRL 55] [QRL 24] [QRL 19]	4.3
Index of average weekly earnings (new series)	All employees all industries and services; manufacturing industries 27 industry groups.	GB	Monthly	[QRL 24]	4.2
Index of average weekly earnings (older series)	All employees, selection of industries and services, 23 industry groups (but some with only partial coverage)	GB	Monthly	[QRL 19] [QRL 24] [QRL 52]	4.2
Index of average weekly earnings (older series)	All employees; all industries and manufacturing industry	GB	Quarterly	[QRL 27]	4.2

(d) Historical statistics

Average weekly earnings and distributions (September)	Adult manual workers, by 58 industries, in 1906	UK	1906	[QRL 18]	7.3
Average weekly earnings (October)	Male and female manual workers, by 40 industries in 1924, 1928, and 1931	UK	1924, 1928, and 1931	[QRL 18]	7.3
Average weekly earnings (October)	Manual workers; men (21 and over), youths and boys, women (18 and over), girls, and all workers, by 15 industries, in 1935	UK	1935	[QRL 18]	7.3
Average weekly and hourly earnings	Adult male and female manual workers in 18–20 main SIC industries, manufacturing and all industries, 1938–68	UK	Biannual	[QRL 18]	7.3

EARNINGS (cont.)
(d) Historical statistics (cont.)

Type of data	Breakdown	Area	Frequency	Publication	Text reference
Average weekly earnings	Manual workers; youths, girls, and part-time women, all industries, 1938–68	UK	Biannual	[QRL 18]	7.3
Average weekly earnings (April)	Industries not covered by main Department of Employment enquiries; manual workers in agriculture, coal-mining, British Rail, inland waterways, London Transport, dock labour, National Health service; 1956–68.	GB and London	Annual	[QRL 18]	5.2.3
Average weekly earnings (October)	Administrative, technical, and clerical employees; males and females; all industries, manufacturing, and 19 industry groups; 1959–68	UK	Annual	[QRL 18]	5.3.2
Average weekly and hourly earnings (May)	Selling staff in large shops by type of shop, age, and sex; 1966–8	GB	Annual	[QRL 18] and December issues of [QRL 24]	5.2.5
Index of average weekly earnings	All employees; all industries and services, manufacturing industries, and 20 industry groups; 1968	GB	Monthly	[QRL 18]	4.2
Indices of average weekly and hourly earnings	Manual workers; all industries and manufacturing; men and women; 1935–68	UK	Biannual	[QRL 18]	7.3
FRINGE BENEFITS					
Fringe benefits, manual workers	Manual workers in 350 companies in 12 industries, by company size and by 19 types of benefit	UK	1960	[QRL 10]	6.2
Fringe benefits, all	Workers in 46 companies, by 11 types of fringe benefit	UK	1971	[QRL 7]	6.2
Fringe benefits	Executives in 230 companies	UK	1970	[QRL 33]	6.2
Fringe benefits, various groups	Various groups	UK	Various	[QRL 42] especially study 127	6.2

Fringe benefits, general	Covered by some salary surveys; see list in Section 5.4	UK	Various	[QRL 39]	5.4
LABOUR COSTS					
Labour costs, 1964	Analysis by 19 main industries and 7 types of cost; also 4 major costs by 5 MLH industries	GB	1964	[QRL 46]	6.3.1
Labour costs, 1968	Analysis by 50 MLH industries and 8 types of cost	GB	1968	[QRL 47] August and December 1970, and January 1971 issues of [QRL 24]	6.3.1
Labour costs, 1968	Same analysis as GB inquiry	Northern Ireland	1968	October issue of [QRL 24]	6.3.1
Labour costs, 1973	Analysis of 9 types of cost by size of firm, for 20 production industries, for operatives and administrative, technical, and clerical workers separately and together	GB	1973	September and October 1975 issues of [QRL 24]	6.3.1
Labour costs, 1975	Analysis of 9 types of cost by size of firm, for 20 production industries, for operatives and administrative, technical, and clerical workers separately and together	GB	1975	September, November, and December issues of [QRL 24]	6.3.1
Labour costs in distribution, insurance, and banking	Analysis of 9 types of cost in wholesale distribution, retail distribution, insurance, banking, and other financial institutions, by size of firm.	GB	1974	June 1976 issue of [QRL 24]	6.3.2
Labour costs per unit of output	For 6 major industrial sectors, manufacturing industries, index of production industries, and for the whole economy	UK	Quarterly	[QRL 24]	6.3.4

QUICK REFERENCE LIST KEY TO PUBLICATIONS

Reference Number	Author/Organization Responsible	Title	Publisher	Frequency or date	Remarks
[QRL 1]	Bowley, A. L.	*Wages and Income in the United Kingdom since 1860*	Cambridge University Press	1937	
[QRL 2]	Crossley, J. R.	'A Monthly Index of Wage Rates by Industry', in *Manchester School of Economics & Social Studies*, vols. xxvii and xxviii		1959 and 1960	Articles on the index appeared in each issue of the journal for these two years apart from the third (September) issue in 1960
[QRL 3]	Dean, A. J. H.	'Earnings in the public and private sectors 1950–1975', in *National Institute Economic Review*, **74**, 60		Nov. 1975	
[QRL 4]	Devons, E., and Crossley, J. R.	*The Guardian Wage Indexes*	The *Guardian*, Manchester	1964	
[QRL 5]	Devons, E, Crossley, J. R., and Maunder, W. F.	'Wage Rate Indexes by Industry 1948–1965' in *Economica*, **39**, 392		Nov. 1968	
[QRL 6]	Mitchell, B., and Deane, P.	*Abstract of British Historical Statistics*	Cambridge University Press	1962	
[QRL 7]	Moonman, J.	*The Effectiveness of Fringe Benefits in Industry*	Gower Press	1973	
[QRL 8]	Ray, G. F.	'Labour costs and international competitiveness' in *National Institute Economic Review*, **61**, 53		Aug. 1972	
[QRL 9]	Ray, G. F.	'Labour costs in OECD countries 1964–1975' in *National Institute Economic Review*, **78**, 58		Nov. 1976	
[QRL 10]	Reid, G. L., and Robertson, D. J. (editors)	*Fringe Benefits, Labour Costs and Social Security*	George Allen & Unwin Ltd, London	1965	
[QRL 11]	CSO	*Abstract of Regional Statistics*	HMSO, London	Annual	

[QRL 12]	Hay–MSL Limited	*Analysis of Managerial Remuneration in the United Kingdom and Overseas*, Background Paper No. 2, Royal Commission on the Distribution of Income & Wealth	HMSO, London	1976	
[QRL 13]	CSO	*Annual Abstract of Statistics*	HMSO, London	Annual	
[QRL 14]	British Transport Commission	*Annual Census of Staff*	HMSO, London	Annually, 1949 to 1962	
[QRL 15]	Inland Revenue	*Annual Report of the Board of Inland Revenue*	HMSO, London	Annually	
[QRL 16]	Civil Service Department	*The British Imperial Calendar and Civil Service List*	HMSO, London	Annually from 1809 to 1973	Replaced by *Civil Service Yearbook*. Formerly published by Stationery Office and Treasury. Information on salary scales appeared from 1925 onwards.
[QRL 17]	British Journal of Industrial Relations	*British Journal of Industrial Relations*	London School of Economics and Political Science	Thrice yearly	
[QRL 18]	Department of Employment	*British Labour Statistics; Historical Abstract 1886—1968*	HMSO, London	1971	
[QRL 19]	Department of Employment	*British Labour Statistics Yearbook*	HMSO, London	Annually since 1969	
[QRL 20]	Business Statistics Office	*Business Monitor*	HMSO, London	Monthly	
[QRL 21]	Department of Employment	*Changes in Rates of Wages and Hours of Work*	HMSO, London	Monthly leaflet	
[QRL 22]	Ministry of Agriculture, Fisheries and Food	*The Changing Structure of the Agricultural Labour Force in England and Wales—Numbers of Workers, Hours, and Earnings*	HMSO, London	1967	
[QRL 23]	Civil Service Department	*Civil Service Yearbook*	HMSO, London	Annually since 1974	
[QRL 24]	Department of Employment	*Department of Employment Gazette*	HMSO, London	Monthly	Formerly *Employment and Productivity Gazette* and *Ministry of Labour Gazette*

Reference Number	Author/Organization Responsible	Title	Publisher	Frequency or date	Remarks
[QRL 25]	Department of Finance, Northern Ireland	Digest of Statistics, Northern Ireland	HMSO, Belfast	Biannual	
[QRL 26]	Welsh Office	Digest of Welsh Statistics	HMSO, Cardiff	Annual	
[QRL 27]	CSO	Economic Trends	HMSO, London	Monthly	
[QRL 28]	CSO	Economic Trends Annual Supplement	HMSO, London	Annual since 1976	Available on subscription
[QRL 29]	British Institute of Management	Employee Benefits Today	British Institute of Management, London	1974	
[QRL 30]	Department of Employment	Family Expenditure Survey	HMSO, London	Annual	
[QRL 31]	Top Salaries Review Board	First Report of Top Salaries Review Board	HMSO, London	1971	
[QRL 32]	National Board for Prices and Incomes	Fifth and Final General Report (No. 170) plus supplement	HMSO, London	1971	
[QRL 33]	British Institute of Management	Fringe Benefits for Executives	British Institute of Management, London	1970	Available on subscription
[QRL 34]	Office of Population Censuses and Surveys	The General Household Survey	HMSO, London	Annual	
[QRL 35]	Office of Population Censuses and Surveys	The General Household Survey; Introductory Report	HMSO, London	1973	
[QRL 36]	Royal Commission on the Distribution of Income and Wealth	Higher Incomes from Employment Report No. 3 of Royal Commission	HMSO, London	1976	
[QRL 37]	Business Statistics Office	Historical Record of the Censuses of Production	HMSO, London	1977	
[QRL 38]	NALGO	Historical Salaries for NALGO and Other Services	NALGO, London	1967	Available on subscription
[QRL 39]	Incomes Data Services	IDS Guide to Salary Surveys	Incomes Data Services Ltd, London	Annual	

[QRL 40]	Incomes Data Services	*IDS International Report*	Incomes Data Services Ltd, London	Fortnightly	
[QRL 41]	Incomes Data Services	*Incomes Data reports*	Incomes Data Services Ltd, London	Fortnightly	
[QRL 42]	Incomes Data Services	*Incomes Data Studies*	Incomes Data Services Ltd, London	Fortnightly	
[QRL 43]	Industrial Relations Services	*Industrial Relations Review and Report*	Industrial Relations Services, London	Fortnightly	
[QRL 44]	Inland Revenue	*Inland Revenue Statistics*	HMSO, London	Annual since 1970	
[QRL 45]	International Labour Office	*Labour Costs in Europe*	International Labour Office, Geneva	1955	
[QRL 46]	Department of Employment and Productivity	*Labour Costs in Great Britain in 1964*	HMSO, London	1968	
[QRL 47]	Department of Employment	*Labour Costs in Great Britain in 1968*	HMSO, London	1971	
[QRL 48]	Labour Research Department	*Labour Research*	Labour Research Department, London	Monthly	Available on subscription
[QRL 49]	London and Cambridge Economic Service	*London and Cambridge Economic Service Bulletin*	Department of Applied Economics, Cambridge	Quarterly	First issued as a monthly bulletin in 1923; ceased publication in 1975
[QRL 50]	British Institute of Management	*Luncheon Vouchers*	British Institute of Management, London	1972	Available on subscription
[QRL 51]	British Institute of Management	*Management Holidays*	British Institute of Management, London	1972	Available on subscription
[QRL 52]	CSO	*Monthly Digest of Statistics*	HMSO, London	Monthly	
[QRL 53]	CSO	*National Income and Expenditure*	HMSO, London	Annual	Commonly known as the 'Blue Book'

Reference Number	Author/Organization Responsible	Title	Publisher	Frequency or date	Remarks
[QRL 54]	National Institute of Economic and Social Research	*National Institute Economic Review*	National Institute of Economic and Social Research, London	Quarterly	
[QRL 55]	Department of Employment	*New Earnings Survey*	HMSO, London	Annually in six parts	
[QRL 56]	Pay Board	*Pay Board Advisory Report 3, Civil Service Science Group*	HMSO, London	1974	
[QRL 57]	Board of Trade Labour Department	*Rates of Wages and Hours of Labour in Various Industries in the UK, 1851–1906*		1908	Unpublished volume
[QRL 58]	Business Statistics Office	*Report on the Census of Distribution*	HMSO, London	5-year intervals to 1976	
[QRL 59]	Business Statistics Office	*Report on the Census of Production*	HMSO, London	Annual	
[QRL 60]	Committee of Inquiry into the Pay of Non-university Teachers	*Report of the Committee of Inquiry into the Pay of Non-University Teachers*	HMSO, London	1974	
[QRL 61]	National Board for Prices and Incomes	*Reports of the National Board for Prices and Incomes*	HMSO, London	Various	1970 reports in period 1966–71
[QRL 62]	Review Body on Armed Forces' Pay	*Pay of Review Body on Armed Forces' Pay*	HMSO, London	Annual since 1972	
[QRL 63]	Review Body on Doctors' and Dentists' Remuneration	*Reports of the Review Body on Doctors' and Dentists' Remuneration*	HMSO, London	Annual since 1971	Earlier Review Body reported twelve times between 1962 and 1970
[QRL 64]	Royal Commission on the Distribution of Income and Wealth Reports	*Reports of the Royal Commission on the Distribution of Income and Wealth*	HMSO, London	Various	First report 1975
[QRL 65]	Top Salaries Review Board	*Reports on Top Salaries*	HMSO, London	Various	First report 1971
[QRL 66]	PER, Synergy, Institute of Personnel Management, Institute of Directors	*Reward*	Synergy Publishing Ltd, Stone, Staffs.	Every 4 months	
[QRL 67]	Royal Commission on Doctors' and Dentists' Remuneration	*Royal Commission on Doctors' and Dentists' Remuneration*	HMSO, London	1960	

[QRL 68]	Department of Education and Science	*Scales of Salaries for Teachers in Establishments of Further Education in England and Wales*	HMSO, London	Annual	
[QRL 69]	Department of Education and Science	*Scales of Salaries for Teachers in Primary and Secondary Schools, England and Wales*	HMSO, London	Annual	
[QRL 70]	Scottish Office	*Scottish Abstract of Statistics*	HMSO, Edinburgh	Annual	
[QRL 71]	Scottish Office	*Scottish Economic Bulletin*	HMSO, Edinburgh	Biannual	
[QRL 72]	Ministry of Labour	*Standard Time Rates*	HMSO, London	Annual	Replaced by *Time Rates of Wages and Hours of Work* [QRL 81]
[QRL 73]	CSO	*Statistical News*	HMSO, London	Quarterly	
[QRL 74]	Department of Education and Science	*Statistics of Education*	HMSO, London	Annual in several volumes	
[QRL 75]	Department of Employment	*Statistics on Incomes, Prices, Employment and Production*	HMSO, London	Quarterly 1962–8	
[QRL 76]	British Institute of Management	*Subsistence and Travelling Expenses in the UK*	British Institute of Management, London	1972	Available on subscription
[QRL 77]	Department of Education and Science	*Survey of Earnings of Qualified Manpower in England and Wales 1966–7*	HMSO, London	1971	Part of *Statistics of Education* series [QRL 74]
[QRL 78]	Institute of Personnel Management	*Survey of Fringe Benefits*	Institute of Personnel Management, London	1966	Available on subscription
[QRL 79]	Inland Revenue	*Survey of Personal Incomes*	HMSO, London	Annual	
[QRL 80]	Transport and General Workers' Union	*TGWU Handbook*	Transport and General Workers' Union, London	1952	Looseleaf updates from 1952 to 1965
[QRL 81]	Department of Employment	*Time Rates of Wages and Hours of Work*	HMSO, London	Annual	
[QRL 82]	Swedish Employers' Confederation	*Wages and Total Labour Costs for Workers—International Survey*	Swedish Employers' Confederation, Stockholm	Annual	

Reference Number	Author/Organization Responsible	Title	Publisher	Frequency or date	Remarks
[QRL 83]	Welsh Office	*Welsh Economic Trends*	HMSO, Cardiff	Annual	
[QRL 84]	International Labour Office	*Yearbook of Labour Statistics*	International Labour Organization, Geneva	Annual	

BIBLIOGRAPHY

[B 1]   Atkinson, A. B., and Harrison, A. J. *Wealth*. Reviews of UK Statistical Sources, Vol. VI, Heinemann Educational Books, London, 1978.
[B 2]   Bayliss, F. J. *British Wages Councils*, Basil Blackwell, Oxford, 1962.
[B 3]   Brown, W., and Terry, M. 'The changing nature of national agreements', *Scottish Journal of Political Economy*, **25**, 119, 1978.
[B 4]   Chapman, A. L., and Knight, R. *Wages and Salaries in the United Kingdom, 1920–1938*, Cambridge University Press, 1953.
[B 5]   Dean, A. J. H. 'Why public sector pay is still a battlefield', *The Guardian*, London, 23 January 1976.
[B 6]   Deane, P., and Cole, W. A. *British Economic Growth, 1688–1955*, Cambridge University Press, 2nd ed., 1969.
[B 7]   Devons, E. *An Introduction to British Economic Statistics*, Cambridge University Press, 1956.
[B 8]   Elliott, R. F. 'The frequency of wage settlements', Aberdeen University Department of Political Economy *Occasional Paper*, 77–18, 1977.
[B 9]   Elliot, R. F. 'The growth of white-collar employment in Great Britain', *British Journal of Industrial Relations*, xv, 39, 1977.
[B 10] Elliott, R. F. 'The national wage round in the United Kingdom; a sceptical view', *Oxford Bulletin of Economics and Statistics*, **38**, 179, 1976.
[B 11] Elliott, R. F. 'Public sector wage movements: 1950–1973', *Scottish Journal of Political Economy*, **24**, 133, 1977.
[B 12] Elliott, R. F., and Bell, D. M. R. 'Wage rates database', Aberdeen University Department of Political Economy, *mimeo*, 1977.
[B 13] Elliott, R. F., and Dean, A. J. H. 'The official wage rates index and the size of wage settlements', *Oxford Bulletin of Economics and Statistics*, **40**, 249, 1978.
[B 14] Elliott, R. F., and Shelton, H. C., 'A wage settlements index for the UK 1950–1975', *Oxford Bulletin of Economics and Statistics*, **40**, 303, 1978.
[B 15] Elliott, R. F., and Steele, R. 'The importance of national wage agreements', *British Journal of Industrial Relations*, xiv, 43, 1976.
[B 16] Fallick, J. L. 'The growth of top salaries in the post-war period', *Industrial Relations*, **8**, 4, 1977.
[B 17] Gilboy, E. W. *Wages in Eighteenth-Century England*, Cambridge, Mass., 1934.
[B 18] Guillebaud, C. W. *The Wages Council System in Great Britain*, Nisbet, 1958.
[B 19] Halsbury. *Report of the Committee of Inquiry into the Pay and Related Conditions of Service of Nurses and Midwives*, HMSO, London, 1974.
[B 20] Hansen, B., and Rehn, G. 'On wage drift; "A problem of money wage dynamics"' in *Twenty Five Essays in Honour of Erik Lindahl*, 1956.
[B 21] Harvey, J. M. *Sources of Statistics*, Clive Bingley, London, 2nd edn., 1969.
[B 22] Kemsley, W. F. F. *Family Expenditure Survey; Handbook on the Sample, Fieldwork and Coding Procedures*, HMSO, London, 1969.
[B 23] Kendall, M. G. (ed.). *Sources and Nature of Statistics of the United Kingdom Volume 1*, Oliver & Boyd, London, 1952.
[B 24] Knowles, K. G. J. C., and Robinson, D. 'Wage rounds and wage policy', *Bulletin of the Oxford University Institute of Statistics*, **24**, 269, 1962.
[B 25] Knowles, K. G. J. C., and Thorne, E. M. F. 'Wage rounds 1948–1959', *Bulletin of the Oxford University Institute of Statistics*, **23**, 1, 1961.
[B 26] Layton, D. *Wages—fog or facts?*, Institute of Economic Affairs, London, 1965.
[B 27] Lydall, H. *The Structure of Earnings*, Oxford University Press, 1968.
[B 28] Marquand, J. *Wage Drift: Origins, Measurement and Behaviour*, Woolwich Polytechnic, London, 1967.
[B 29] Mulvey, C. 'Collective agreements and relative earnings in the UK in 1973', *Economica*, **43**, 419, 1976.
[B 30] Oliver, F. R. 'The general household survey', *Social and Economic Administration*, **8**, 64, 1974.

[B 31] Phelps Browne, H., and Browne, M. *A Century of Pay*, Macmillan, 1968.

[B 32] Reynolds, L. G., and Taft, C. H. *The Evolution of Wage Structure*, Yale University Press, 1956.

[B 33] Routh, G. C. *Occupation and Pay in Great Britain 1906–1960*, Cambridge University Press, 1965.

[B 34] Stark, T. *Personal Incomes*. Reviews of UK Statistical Sources, Vol. VI, Heinemann Educational Books, London, 1978.

[B 35] Whitehead, F. *Social security statistics* in Reviews of United Kingdom Statistical Sources Vol. II, Heinemann Educational Books, London, 1974.

[B 36] Wigham, E. *Strikes and the Government*, Macmillan, 1976.

[B 37] Department of Employment, *Codot Directory*, HMSO, London, 1972.

[B 38] Interdepartmental Committee on Social and Economic Research. *Guides to Official Sources: No. 1. Labour Statistics*, HMSO, London, 1948.

[B 39] Interdepartmental Committee on Social and Economic Research. *Guides to Official Sources: No. 1. Labour Statistics,* HMSO, London, revised edn., 1958.

[B 40] Central Statistical Office. *Guide to Official Statistics*, HMSO, London, 1976.

[B 41] Estimates Committee. *Report on the Government Statistical Services*, HMSO, London, 1966.

[B 42] General Register Office. *Sample Census 1966 (Great Britain) Economic Activity Tables*, HMSO, London, 1968.

[B 43] Pay Board. *Special Report on the Relative Pay of Mineworkers*, HMSO, London, 1974.

[B 44] Office of Manpower Economics. *Wage Drift*, HMSO, London, 1973.

APPENDICES

APPENDIX A. Numbers of workers covered by principal national collective agreements.

Industry/Agreement	Area	Estimated coverage
Forestry and fishing		
Forestry Commission	GB	5,300
Trawler fishing	GB	10,000
Mining and quarrying		
Coal mining: underground and surface workers (including craftsmen)—NCB	GB	265,000
Roadstone quarrying	GB	10,000
Quarrying	NI	5,000
Sand and gravel industry	GB	10,000
Food, drink and tobacco		
Flour milling (mill operatives)	GB	7,500
Baking		
national agreement for multiple bakers	E & W	35,000
national agreement for master bakers private and co-operative	E & W	13,000
	Scotland	11,500
Biscuit manufacture	GB	38,500
Bacon curing	GB	14,000
	NI	2,000
Milk, milk products manufacture and processing	E & W	30,000
Milk processing	NI	2,500
Beet sugar manufacture	GB	5,000
Cocoa, chocolate and sugar confectionery	GB	45,000
Corn trade:		
mill and other manual workers (excluding transport workers)	GB	13,500
transport workers	GB	9,500
Seed crushing, compound and provender manufacture	UK	6,500
Food manufacture	GB	70,000
Brewing	Scotland and one brewery in Newcastle upon Tyne	7,500
Tobacco manufacture	UK	38,500
Coal and petroleum products		
Coke and by-products—NCB	GB	6,000
Chemicals and allied industries		
Heavy chemicals (firms affiliated to the Chemical Industries Association):		
all workers excluding maintenance craftsmen and building operatives	GB	50,000
maintenance craftsmen	GB	12,000
British Nuclear Fuels Ltd	UK	5,500
Drug and fine chemicals manufacture	GB	18,000
Paint, varnish and lacquer manufacture	GB	20,000
Soap, candle and edible fat manufacture	GB	13,000
Surgical dressings manufacture	GB	7,000
Metal manufacture		
Pig iron manufacture	E & W and certain works in Scotland	14,000
Iron and steel manufacture:		
steel melting shops and rolling mills	E & W and certain works in Scotland	67,000
maintenance craftsmen	E & W and certain works in Scotland	26,000
sheet rolling mills	E & W and certain works in Scotland	6,750
Sheffield shift	Sheffield	9,500
Light castings manufacture	GB	40,000
Brass and copper rolling and casting	West Midlands	6,000
Brassworking and founding	GB	54,000
Mechanical engineering		
Engineering (federated firms only)	UK (except South West Wales)	1,250,000*
Engineering	South West Wales	5,000
Agricultural machinery	GB	20,000
Electrical engineering		
Electrical cable making industry (firms covered by the Joint Industrial Council)	GB	23,500
Shipbuilding and marine engineering		
Shipbuilding and ship repairing	UK	110,000
Vehicles		
Vehicle building	UK	26,000
Railway workshops—British Rail	GB	50,000
Railway wagon repairing—private firms	GB	5,000
Metal goods not elsewhere specified		
Lighter metal trades	Sheffield	5,000
Cutlery and silverware trade	Sheffield	7,000
Wire and wire rope industries	GB	15,000
Tin box manufacture	GB	25,000
Lock, latch and key making	England	9,000
Textiles		
Cotton spinning and weaving	Lancs, Cheshire, Yorks and Derbyshire	70,000
Flax preparing and spinning	NI	4,250
Silk manufacture	UK (excluding Macclesfield)	9,000
Knitting, sewing threads, dyeing, printing and finishing, small wares, throwing and making up	Leek	5,000
Linen weaving	NI	3,000
Wool textile:		
operatives	Yorks	80,000
operatives	Scotland	9,000
Jute preparing, spinning and weaving	Dundee	8,000
Knitting industries federation	Midlands	81,000
Knitwear manufacture	Scotland (excluding Hawick)	10,000
	Hawick	5,000
Carpet manufacture	GB	35,000
Narrow woven fabrics	UK	9,000
Textile bleaching, dyeing, printing and finishing	GB	18,500
Hosiery finishing industry	Midlands	8,250
Leather, leather goods and fur		
Leather production	GB	19,000
Leather goods and allied trades	GB	18,000
Clothing and footwear		
Glove making	E & W	6,000
Footwear manufacture	UK (except East Lancs and the Fylde coast)	65,000
	East Lancs and the Fylde coast	10,000

* It is estimated that non-federated firms with about 750,000 manual workers also follow the engineering agreement.

Industry/Agreement	Area	Estimated coverage
Bricks, pottery, glass, cement, etc		
Refractory goods manufacture	E & W	7,500
Building brick and allied industries	E & W	23,500
Fletton brick manufacture	Beds, Bucks and Peterborough	8,500
Pottery manufacture	GB	45,000
Glass container manufacture	GB	18,000
Cement manufacture (excluding maintenance craftsmen)	UK	7,000
Asbestos cement manufacture	GB	5,000
Cast stone and cast concrete products	E & W	22,500
Timber, furniture, etc		
Home grown timber trade	E & W	10,000
Sawmilling	E & W	27,000
Furniture manufacture	GB	80,000
Upholstery and bedding filling materials	GB	5,500
Bedding manufacture	GB	13,000
Timber container industry	E & W and NI	14,000
Paper, printing and publishing		
Paper and board making	UK	54,000
Fibreboard packing case making	UK	19,000
Carton manufacture	GB	12,500
Manufactured stationery	E & W	12,000
National newspapers	London	22,000
General printing, bookbinding and periodical and newspaper production (excluding national newspapers)	England and Wales (except London)	120,000
	Scotland	15,000
Lithographic printing and photogravure	London	43,000
	E & W	19,000
Other manufacturing industries		
Rubber manufacture	GB	65,000
Plastics mouldings and fabricating	GB	10,000
Construction		
Building	GB	768,000
Road transport in building	E & W	16,000
Building and civil engineering	NI	46,500
Local authorities	Scotland	11,000
Civil engineering	GB	85,000
Constructional engineering	GB	175,000
Mastic asphalt laying	GB	20,000
Electrical contracting	E & W	50,000
Heating and ventilating	GB	10,000
Painting	Scotland	45,000
Thermal insulating	GB	12,000
Plumbing	E & W	8,000
	Scotland and NI	20,000
Gas, electricity and water		
Gas supply (workers other than maintenance craftsmen)	GB	45,500
Electricity supply (except British Rail)	GB	110,500
Electricity supply	NI	3,500
Water supply (workers other than skilled engineering and building craftsmen)	E & W	22,000
Transport and communication		
Railway service—BR (conciliation and miscellaneous grades)	GB	122,000
National Carriers Ltd/Freightliners Ltd	GB	14,500
Railway service—London Transport Executive (conciliation and miscellaneous grades)	London	12,000
Road passenger transport:		
company-owned buses	GB	80,000
municipal omnibus undertakings	GB	26,000
London Transport Executive drivers and conductors	London	20,500
maintenance staff and garages	London	6,000
Coach drivers (private hire)	SW England	5,000
Road haulage workers	NI	5,000
British Road Services (operating and ancillary grades)	GB	18,000
Road freight	NI	2,500
Merchant Navy	UK	50,000
Dock labour (and coal trimmers)	GB	34,500
BOAC and BEA—engineering and maintenance grades	UK	10,000
Post Office:		
manipulative grades	UK	201,000
engineering grades	UK	116,000
Cold storage	GB	5,000
Distributive trades		
Wholesale grocery and provision trade	E & W	25,000
Slaughtering	E & W	5,000
Retail multiple grocery and provision trade	E & W	100,000
	Scotland	12,000
Retail distribution (CWS)	GB	200,000
Milk distribution	E & W	9,000
Retail meat trade	E & W	50,000
	Scotland	7,000
Retail multiple footwear trade	GB	44,500
Retail pharmacy	E & W	48,500
Coal and coke distribution	GB (excluding London)	50,000
Iron, steel and non-ferrous scrap	GB	20,000
Professional and scientific services		
Local authorities services (school meals services)	E & W	250,700
Health services		
domestic and similar grades of ancillary workers	GB	230,000
craftsmen and semi-skilled engineering workers	GB	11,000
building operatives	GB	9,250
UK Atomic Energy Authority	UK	7,250
Dentistry technicians	GB	7,000
Miscellaneous services		
Cinema theatres	UK	25,000
Catering (British Transport hotels)	GB	11,000
Motor vehicle retail and repair industry	UK	367,500
Public administration and defence		
Civil service non-industrial grades	UK	11,000
Prison service	GB	13,000
Government industrial establishments	UK	193,000
Local authorities services	E & W	
Manual and semi-skilled grades	E & W	573,500
Engineering craftsmen and electricians	Scotland	13,000
Manual workers	E & W	88,000
River authorities	UK	5,000
Police force	UK	115,000
Fire brigades	GB	23,000

Source: November 1973 Department of Employment Gazette

APPENDIX B

NATIONAL BOARD FOR PRICES AND INCOMES PUBLISHED REPORTS

Report No.	Reference	Gazetted (i.e. formally referred)	Published	Cmnd. No.
1.	Road Haulage Rates (Interim)	6.5.65	28.6.65	2695
2.	Wages, Costs and Prices in the Printing Industry	18.5.65	17.8.65	2750
3.	Prices of Bread and Flour	6.5.65	1.9.65	2760
4.	Prices of Household and Toilet Soaps, Soap Powders and Soap Flakes, and Soapless Detergents	6.5.65	11.10.65	2791
5.	Remuneration of Administrative and Clerical Staff in the Electricity Supply Industry	16.6.65	25.10.65	2801
6.	Salaries of Midland Bank Staff	17.6.65	24.11.65	2839
7.	Electricity and Gas Tariffs—London Electricity Board and Scottish, South Western and Wales Gas Board	18.6.65 +20.10.65	22.12.65	2862
8.	Pay and Conditions of Service of British Railways Staff (Conciliation, Salaried and Workshop Grades)	15.10.65	14.1.65	2873
9.	Wages in the Bakery Industry (First Report)	3.12.65	19.1.66	2878
10.	Armed Forces Pay	25.11.65	28.1.66	2881
11.	Pay of the Higher Civil Service	25.11.65	28.1.66	2882
12.	Coal Prices	20.12.65	24.2.66	2919
13.	Costs, Prices and Profits in the Brewing Industry	26.1.66	19.4.66	2965
14.	Road Haulage Charges (Final Report)	6.5.65	21.4.66	2968
15.	Scottish Teachers' Salaries	24.1.66	24.5.66	3005
16.	Pay and Conditions of Busmen	4.3.66	26.5.66	3012
17.	Wages in the Bakery Industry (Final Report)	3.12.65	9.6.66	3019
18.	Pay of Industrial Civil Servants	21.10.65	21.6.66	3034
19.	General Report, April 1965 to July 1966	—	23.8.66	3087
20.	Laundry and Dry Cleaning Charges	4.1.66	7.9.66	3093
21.	Coal Distribution Costs	7.3.66	7.9.66	3094
22.	Rate of Interest on Building Society Mortgages	24.5.66	14.11.66	3136
23.	Productivity and Pay during the Period of Severe Restraint	24.8.66	15.12.66	3167
24.	Wages and Condition in the Electrical Contracting Industry	1.7.66	22.12.66	3172
25.	Pay of Workers in Agriculture in England and Wales	16.12.66	2.2.67	3199
26.	Prices of Standard Newsprint	8.12.66	23.2.67	3210
27.	Pay of Workers in the Retail Drapery, Outfitting and Footwear Trades	16.12.66	9.3.67	3224
	Pay of Workers in the Retail Drapery, Outfitting and Footwear Trades: Statistical Supplement	—	18.4.67	3224–1
28.	Prices of Compound Fertilisers	8.12.66	13.3.67	3228
29.	The Pay and Conditions of Manual Workers in Local Authorities, the National Health Service Gas and Water Supply	6.8.66	16.3.67	3230
	The Pay and Conditions of Manual Workers in Local Authorities, the National Health Service, Gas and Water Supply: Statistical Supplement	—	4.5.67	3230–1
30.	Pay and Conditions of Limbfitters employed by J. E. Hanger and Co	9.1.67	6.4.67	3245
31.	Distribution Costs of Fresh Fruit and Vegetables	3.10.66	26.4.67	3265
32.	Fire Service Pay	19.12.66	16.5.67	3287
33.	The Remuneration of Milk Distributors (Interim Report)	13.1.67	23.5.67	3294
34.	Bank Charges	22.6.66	24.5.67	3292
35.	Pay and Conditions of Merchant Navy Officers	26.4.67	2.6.67	3302
36.	Productivity Agreements	24.8.66	13.6.67	3311
37.	Costs and Charges in the Motor Repairing and Servicing Industry	24.8.66	8.8.67	3368
38.	Portland Cement Prices	24.2.67	10.8.67	3381
39.	Costs and Prices of Aluminium Semi-Manufactures	24.8.66	11.8.67	3378
40.	Second General Report July 1966 to August 1967	—	31.8.67	3394
41.	Salaries of Staff employed by the General Accident Fire and Life Assurance Corporation Ltd	9.6.67	7.9.67	3398
42.	Pay of Electricity Supply Workers	11.8.67	19.9.67	3405
43.	Costs and Revenue of National Daily Newspapers	27.7.67	19.10.67	3435
44.	London Weighting in the Non-Industrial Civil Service	21.3.67	2.11.67	3436
45.	Pay of Chief and Senior Officers (1) in Local Government Service and (2) in the Greater London Council	(1) 6.12.66 (2) 29.11.66	23.11.67	3473
46.	The Remuneration of Milk Distributors (Final Report)	17.1.67	28.11.67	3477
47.	Prices of Fletton and Non-Fletton Bricks	26.5.67	30.11.67	3480
48.	Charges, Costs and Wages in the Road Haulage Industry	18.8.67	6.12.67	3482
	Statistical Supplement:	—	8.3.68	3482–1

Report No.	Reference	Gazetted (i.e. formally referred)	Published	Cmnd. No.
49.	Pay and Conditions of Service of Workers in the Engineering Industry (First Report on the Engineering Industry)	16.5.67	19.12.67	3495
	Statistical Supplement: Pay and Conditions of Staff Workers in the Engineering Industry	—	6.3.68	3495-1
50.	Productivity Agreements in the Bus Industry	25.7.67	21.12.67	3498
51.	Pay and Productivity of Industrial Employees of the United Kingdom Atomic Energy Authority	17.10.67	2.1.68	3499
52.	Costs and Charges in the Radio and Television Rental and Relay Industry	26.1.67	25.1.68	3520
53.	Flour Prices	12.1.68	1.2.68	3522
54.	Remuneration of Solicitors	10.2.67	8.2.68	3529
55.	Distributors' Margins in Relation to Manufacturers' Recommended Prices	28.12.67	22.2.68	3546
56.	Proposals by the London Transport Board for fare increases in the London Area	5.10.67	7.3.68	3561
57.	Gas Prices (First Report)	5.10.67	18.3.68	3567
58.	Post Office Charges	5.10.67	18.3.68	3574
59.	Bulk Supply Tariff of the Central Electricity Generating Board	5.10.67	18.3.68	3575
60.	Pay of Nurses and Midwives in the National Health Service	30.6.67	28.3.68	3585
61.	Prices of Secondary Batteries	13.2.68	10.4.68	3597
62.	Increases in Rents of Local Authority Housing	12.12.67	25.4.68	3604
	Increases in Rents of Local Authority Housing: Statistical Supplement	—	1.10.68	3604-1
63.	Pay of Municipal Busmen	27.1.68	26.4.68	3605
64.	Increase in Prices in Mercury Hearing Aid Batteries manufactured by Mallory Batteries Ltd	13.2.68	13.5.68	3625
65.	Payment by Results Systems	23.3.67	14.5.68	3627
	Payments by Results Systems (Supplement)	—	10.12.68	3627-1
66.	Price of Butyl Rubber	16.2.68	13.5.68	3626
67.	Passenger Fares and Freight Charges of the North of Scotland, Orkney and Shetland Shipping Company Ltd	30.1.68	16.5.68	3631
68.	Agreement made between certain Engineering Firms' and Draughtsmens' and Allied Technicians' Association	20.2.68	16.5.68	3632
69.	Pay and Conditions of Busmen Employed by the Corporation of Belfast, Glasgow and Liverpool	1.3.68	23.5.68	3646
70.	Standing Reference on the Pay of the Armed Forces	2.11.67	30.5.68	3651
71.	Architects' Costs and Fees	11.4.67	29.5.68	3653
72.	Proposed Increases by British Railways Board in certain Country-wide Fares and Charges	5.10.67	30.5.68	3656

Report No.	Reference	Gazetted (i.e. formally referred)	Published	Cmnd. No.
73.	The Prices of Hoover Domestic Appliances	13.2.68	8.6.68	3671
74.	Agreement relating to Terms and Conditions of Employment of Staff employed by the Prudential and Pearl Assurance Companies	22.3.68	21.6.68	3674
75.	Costs and Prices of the Chocolate and Sugar Confectionery Industry	4.1.68	3.7.68	3694
76.	Increase in Rental Charges for the Equipment hired from IBM UK Ltd	11.4.68	10.7.68	3699
77.	Third General Report August 1967 to July 1968	—	25.7.68	3715
78.	Award Relating to Terms and Conditions of Employment in the Road Passenger Transport Department of Rochdale County Borough Council	30.5.68	26.7.68	3723
79.	National Guidelines Covering Productivity Payments in the Electricity Supply Industry	3.5.68	30.7.68	3726
80.	Distributors' Margins on Paint, Childrens' Clothing, Household Textiles and Proprietary Medicines	14.5.68	13.8.68	3737
81.	Pay Awards made by the City and County of Bristol to staff employed in its dock undertaking	30.5.68	23.8.68	3752
82.	Pay on an Agreement relating to the Pay of Sawyers and Woodcutting Machinists in the Sawmilling Industry	21.6.68	20.9.68	3768
83.	Job Evaluation	23.3.67	29.9.68	3772
	Job Evaluation (Supplement)		10.12.68	3772-1
84.	Report on a Settlement relating to the Pay of certain workers employed in the Thermal Insulation Contracting industry	16.8.68	8.10.68	3784
85.	Pay and Conditions of Busmen employed by the Corporation of Dundee	13.8.68	15.10.68	3791
86.	Pay of Staff Workers in the Gas Industry	25.7.68	24.10.68	3795
87.	Proposed Increase in London Taxicab Fares	28.6.68	25.10.68	3796
88.	Pay of Pilots employed by the British Overseas Airways Corporation	31.5.68	29.10.68	3789
89.	Office Staff Employment Agencies Charges and Salaries	22.3.68	14.11.68	3828
90.	Pay of Vehicle Maintenance Workers in British Road Services	27.8.68	4.12.68	3848
91.	Pay and Conditions in the Civil Engineering Industry	31.5.68	28.11.68	3836
92.	Pay and Conditions in the Building Industry	31.5.68	28.11.68	3837
93.	Pay and Conditions in the Construction Industry other than Building and Civil Engineering	31.5.68	28.11.68	3838
	Statistical Supplement: Reports Nos. 91, 92 and 93 (Supplement). Pay and Conditions in the Building Industry, the Civil Engineering Industry, and the Construction Industry other than Building and Civil Engineering	—	1.4.69	3982

Report No.	Reference	Gazetted (i.e. formally referred)	Published	Cmnd. No.
94.	Productivity Agreements in the Road Haulage Industry	13.8.68	5.12.68	3847
95.	Pay and Conditions of Busmen employed by the Corporation of Wigan	10.9.68	6.12.68	3845
96.	Pay of Busmen employed by the Corporation of Great Yarmouth	10.9.68	6.12.68	3844
97.	Distributors' Costs and Margins on Furniture, Domestic Electrical Appliances and Footwear	17.8.67	17.12.68	3858
98.	Standing Reference on the Pay of University Teachers in Great Britain (First Report)	2.11.67	18.12.68	3866
99.	Pay of Maintenance Workers Employed by Bus Companies	13.9.68	2.1.69	3868
100.	Synthetic Organic Dyestuffs and Organic Pigments Prices	19.9.68	28.1.69	3895
101.	Pay of Workers in Agriculture in England and Wales	3.1.69	30.1.69	3911
102.	Gas Prices (Second Report)	5.10.67	13.2.69	3924
103.	Pay and Productivity in the Car Delivery Industry	8.10.68	18.2.69	3929
104.	Pay and Conditions of Service of Engineering Workers (Second Report on the Engineering Industry)	16.5.67	20.2.69	3931
105.	Pay of General Workers and Craftsmen in Imperial Chemical Industries Ltd	28.11.68	25.2.69	3941
106.	Pay in the London Clearing Banks	29.11.68	28.2.69	3943
107.	Top Salaries in the Private Sector and Nationalised Industries	2.7.68	25.3.69	3970
108.	Pay and Conditions in the Electrical Contracting Industry in Scotland	24.12.68	20.3.69	3966
109.	Pay of Salaried Staff in Imperial Chemical Industries Ltd	31.12.68	28.3.69	3981
110.	Pay and Conditions in the Clothing Manufacturing Industries	1.10.68	17.4.69	4002
	Pay and Conditions in the Clothing Manufacturing Industries (Supplement)	—	17.7.69	4002–1
111.	Steel Prices	24.12.68	21.5.69	4033
112.	Proposals by the London Transport Board for Fares Increases	20.2.69	15.5.69	4036
113.	Manufacturers' Prices of Toilet Preparations	24.12.68	3.6.69	4066
114.	Pay and duties of Light-Keepers	28.2.69	4.6.69	4067
115.	Journalists' Pay	11.3.69	10.6.69	4077
116.	Standing Reference on the Pay of the Armed Forces (Second Report)	2.11.67	16.6.69	4079
117.	Pay and Conditions of Workers in the Exhibition Contracting Industry	18.3.69	18.6.69	4088
118.	Prices of Non-Alloy Bright Steel Bars	7.3.69	19.6.69	4093
119.	Man-made Fibre and Cotton Yarn Prices (First Report)	20.2.69	19.6.69	4092
120.	Pay and Conditions in the Electrical Contracting Industry	13.12.68	27.6.69	4097
121.	Post Office Charges: Inland Parcel Post and Remittance Services	16.5.69	15.7.69	4115
122.	Fourth General Report July 1968 to July 1969	—	29.7.69	4130
123.	Productivity Agreements	26.11.68	5.8.69	4136
124.	Coal Prices	22.5.69	21.8.69	4149
125.	Salaries of certain staff employed by BICC Ltd	27.6.69	24.9.69	4168
126.	Remuneration of workers in Smithfield Market	24.4.69	9.10.69	4171
127.	Man-made Fibre and Cotton Yarn Prices (Second Report)	20.2.69	17.10.69	4180
128.	Pay of Ground Staff at Aerodromes	11.4.69	28.10.69	4182
129.	Pay of Pilots employed by BOAC	5.6.69	4.11.69	4197
130.	Plasterboard Prices	5.8.69	5.11.69	4184
131.	Pay of certain employees in the Film Processing Industry	8.8.69	6.11.69	4185
132.	Salary Structures	25.7.68	18.11.69	4187
133.	Portland Cement Prices	15.8.69	12.11.69	4215
134.	Standing Reference on the Remuneration of Solicitors (First Report)	13.3.69	19.11.69	4217
135.	Pay Structure within HM Stationery Office	5.8.69	21.11.69	4219
136.	Beer Prices	24.4.69	28.11.69	4227
137.	Proposals by the British Railways Board for fare increases in the London Commuter Area	22.8.69	22.12.69	4250
138.	Coal Prices (First Report)	18.11.69	2.1.70	4255
139.	Electric Motor Prices	7.10.69	6.1.70	4258
140.	Pay and Conditions of Workers in the Milk Industry	22.7.69	22.1.70	4267
141.	Costs and Revenue of National Newspapers	19.9.69	5.2.70	4277
142.	Standing Reference of the Pay of the Armed Forces (Third Report)	2.11.67	25.2.70	4291
143.	Hours and Overtime in the London Clearing Banks	28.11.69	27.2.70	4301
144.	Bread Prices and Pay in the Baking Industry (First Report)	6.1.70	7.4.70	4329
145.	Standing Reference on the Pay of University Teachers in Great Britain (Second Report)	2.11.67	9.4.70	4334
146.	Pay and Conditions of Industrial Civil Servants	7.10.69	29.4.70	4351
147.	Margarine and Compound Cooking Fats	3.2.70	14.5.70	4368
148.	Prices of Primary Batteries proposed by the Ever Ready Company (Great Britain) Ltd	24.2.70	19.5.70	4370

Report No.	Reference	Gazetted (i.e. formally referred)	Published	Cmnd. No.
149.	Pay and other terms and conditions of employment of workers in the Pottery Industry	24.10.69	21.7.70	4411
150.	Pay and other terms and conditions of employment in the Fletton Brick Industry and the prices charged by the London Brick Company	27.1.70	23.7.70	4422
151.	Bread Prices and pay in the Baking Industry	6.1.70	28.7.70	4428
152.	Pay and Productivity in the Water Supply Industry	27.1.70	4.8.70	4434
153.	Coal Prices (Second Report)	18.11.69	13.8.70	4455
	Coal Prices (Second Report) (Supplement)	—	27.4.71	4455-1
	Coal Prices (Second Report) (Supplement)	—	27.4.71	4455-2
154.	Tea prices	14.5.70	14.8.70	4456
155.	Costs and efficiency in the Gas Industry	20.1.70	19.8.70	4458
156.	Costs and Revenues of Independent Television Companies	31.3.70	29.10.70	4524
157.	Standing Reference on the Pay of the Armed Forces (Fourth Report)—The Pay of Senior Officers	2.11.67	8.12.70	4513
158.	Standing Reference on the Pay of the Armed Forces (Fifth Report)—Separation Allowance	2.11.67	12.11.70	4529
159.	London Transport Fares	28.5.70	26.11.70	4540
160.	Costs, prices and profitability in the Ice-Cream manufacturing industry	16.6.70	3.12.70	4548
161.	Hours of Work, Overtime and Shiftworking	29.4.69	30.12.70	4554
	Hours of Work, Overtime and Shiftworking (Supplement)	—	30.12.70	4554-1
162.	Costs, charges and Productivity of the National Freight Corporation	9.6.70	13.1.71	4569
163.	Costs and charges in the Motor Repair and Servicing Industry	11.6.70	16.2.71	4590
164.	Standing Reference on the Remuneration of Solicitors (Second Report)	13.3.69	1.4.71	4624
165.	Prices, Profits and Costs in Food Distribution	29.5.70	20.4.71	4645
166.	Pay and Conditions of Service of Ancillary Workers in National Health Service Hospitals	22.5.70	28.4.71	4644
167.	Pay and Conditions of Service of Workers in the Laundry and Dry Cleaning Industry	22.5.70	28.4.71	4647
168.	Pay and Conditions in the Contract Cleaning Trade	22.5.70	28.4.71	4637
169.	General Problems of Low Pay	—	28.4.71	4648
170.	Fifth and Final General Report July 1969 to March 1971	—	29.4.71	4649
	Fifth and Final General Report (Supplement)	—	29.4.71	4649-1

APPENDIX C

WS 62

MONTHLY RETURN OF TOTAL WAGES AND SALARIES

Department of Employment
Statistics Division A4
Orphanage Road
Watford WD1 1PJ

Tel. No. Watford 28500
Ext 408

(Date as postmark)

These numbers should be quoted
in any correspondence

STATISTICS OF TRADE ACT, 1947

Dear Sir(s),

Notice under Section 1

    This is to give you notice that the Secretary of State for Employment requires you, if your company or organisation employs 25 persons or more in all (i.e. including operatives and other manual workers as well as administrative, technical and clerical employees), to furnish the information asked for overleaf, which is required for compiling monthly indices of average earnings of employees for use in the appreciation of economic trends.

    When the figures for the appropriate month have been entered, the form should be returned to the Director of Statistics (S.A.4), Department of Employment, Orphanage Road, Watford, WD1 1PJ, in the enclosed envelope as soon as possible and in any case not later than the 10th of the month following that to which the figures relate. Each month, after extraction of information for processing, the form will be returned to you for use in the following month.

    If your company or organisation employs fewer than 25 persons, the return need not be completed in full, but should be noted with the number employed, signed and returned to the above address in the enclosed envelope.

    The information furnished will be regarded as strictly confidential and care will be taken that, in any statistics published, figures relating to individual firms or undertakings will not be disclosed.

Yours faithfully

A R Thatcher

Director of Statistics

NOTES FOR GUIDANCE IN COMPLETING THE FORM OVERLEAF

1   **Employees paid weekly**

Entries in columns (2) and (3) should cover all employees (both full-time and part-time and both wage-earners and salary-earners) in Great Britain who are paid weekly and received some remuneration in the last pay-week in the relevant month.

2   **Employees paid monthly or four-weekly**

Entries in columns (4) and (5) should cover all employees (both full-time and part-time and both wage-earners and salary-earners) in Great Britain who are paid monthly or four-weekly and received some remuneration in the relevant monthly period. When there are two pay days during the calendar month for those paid four-weekly, give figures for the second one.

3   **Employees paid at other intervals**

Information is not required about employees paid at quarterly or other intervals. However, if substantial numbers of employees are paid fortnightly, arrangements for their inclusion in the return may be made in consultation with the Department.

4   **Total wages and salaries**

Entries in columns (2) and (4) should be the total gross wages and salaries paid to the employees concerned in the periods stated, including overtime payments, bonuses (including annual and other periodical bonuses), non-contractual gifts, commission, etc., before any deductions are made for income tax, employees' national insurance contributions and employees' contributions to pension funds, etc. Redundancy pay and employers' contributions to national insurance, pension schemes, etc. should not be included. Fees paid to directors are not to be included.

5   **Holiday pay paid in advance to weekly-paid employees**

Where possible, the amount to be entered in column (2) should exclude holiday pay paid in advance for holidays outside the pay-week. Where this is not possible, enter an approximate estimate of such payments in column (2a).

6   **General**

Column (7) headed "Remarks" may be used, when appropriate, for brief explanations of unusual changes in the figures.

APPENDIX D.   *The 1978 NES questionnaire*

REPORT   A 50   NEW EARNINGS SURVEY 1978

Covering letter to the employer

Dear Sir(s)

NEW EARNINGS SURVEY, 1978

As in previous years, the Department is making a survey of the earnings of a relatively small sample of individual employees to provide the essential minimum of statistical information which is needed by the Government and is not available from other sources.

The questionnaire is being kept as simple and short as practicable. It is essentially the same as that used last year except for the omission of a question on types of incentive payments and its replacement by a question on types of collective agreement which was last asked in the 1973 survey.

It is very important that forms should be completed for everyone in the sample, and so the information is being asked for under the Statistics of Trade Act, 1947. The formal statutory notice of requirement will be found overleaf. The sample comprises those employees whose national insurance numbers end in certain digits; it therefore includes those who were in the 1977 sample and are still in employment.

A form is enclosed for completion for each employee in the sample who is in your employment. Please provide information only about the employee named on the perforated tear-off slip at the top of the form, even though the individual may not seem typical and even though you may not be the employee's main employer.

If the named person is in one of the following categories, there is no need to complete the details. So that we need not trouble you further, please endorse the form to show to which category this person belongs and return it as indicated below:—

— a private domestic servant,
— one of your former employees now retired and receiving an occupational pension,
— a wife working for, or assisting, her husband or a husband working for his wife,
— a person employed outside the United Kingdom,
— a person who left your employment before 1st March 1978.
— a company director who does not receive a salary.

All the information on the completed forms will be treated as strictly confidential, and under no circumstances will statistics relating to any identifiable individual or firm be published. Neither the name nor the address of either the employee or the employer is recorded on the magnetic tapes which are used for computer processing of the survey information.

If the employee's workplace is in Northern Ireland, we should be grateful if you would complete the return and agree to its transfer to the Department of Manpower Services, Belfast, for inclusion in their corresponding survey of employees in Northern Ireland. Please enter Northern Ireland and the town or district in reply to question 8.

I should be grateful if you would return the endorsed or completed forms within the next month to the local office of the Department at the address shown at the head of this letter. A franked addressed label is enclosed. Exceptionally, if you prefer, the forms may be sent direct to the Department of Employment Statistics Division A5, Orphanage Road, Watford, Herts. WD1 1PJ. The staff at the local office of the Department or at the Watford address (telephone: Watford 28500, Ext 530 or 578) will be pleased to do all they can to help, if you have any questions on detailed points.

If you need a little longer to complete the form, please consult that local office. We are being pressed to get the survey results out as early as possible and so prompt returns will be appreciated.

An extensive range of analyses of the results of the survey is published each year in a series of booklets, with a selection of key results in the *Department of Employment Gazette* in October. If you would like to know more about the statistical information available from the survey, please do not hesitate to get in touch with us at the Watford address.

Yours faithfully,

Director of Statistics

STATISTICS OF TRADE ACT 1947

Notice under Section 1

This is to give you notice that the Secretary of State for Employment requires you to furnish the information asked for in respect of the employee(s) named on the enclosed form(s). The information is needed to provide statistics of the earnings of various groups of employees and other related matters as part of a statistical service for industry and Government Departments.

PARTICULARS OF EMPLOYEE FOR WHOM INFORMATION IS REQUIRED

Surname and initials   Mr/Mrs/Miss ....

Works No., Branch, Dept., Contract, etc. ....

(Please detach this part before returning the form)

CONFIDENTIAL   **Department of Employment — New Earnings Survey 1978**

	FOR OFFICIAL USE	
address stamp		Sheet ....Line ....

B/Seq No.	
NI No.	[ ][ ][ ][ ][ ][ ] 1 4
MLH	

Please provide the following information about the employment, earnings and hours of the employee named above **for the pay-week (or other longer period used for pay purposes) which included Wednesday, 12th April 1978.**

If the employee was not in your employment at any time during the pay-period which included 12th April, please give information for another pay-period ending after 28th February 1978.

✻ Please answer questions marked ✻ by putting a circle round the number to the right of the answer which applies. (e.g. In answer to question 1(a) put ① for a weekly-paid employee but ⑥ for a monthly-paid employee).

1. Total earnings for the specified period

✻(a)   Please indicate the length of the period to which the earnings entered ✻(a) at (c) below relate.

> one week 1   two weeks 2   three weeks 3
> four weeks 4   five weeks 5   one calendar month 6
> other period (please specify) 7

✻(b)   Were the employee's earnings for this particular period affected by
— sickness absence
— other absence (ignore losses of overtime)
— holidays
— short-time working
— or the employment lasting for only part of the period?

✻(b)   earnings affected 1
earnings not affected .2

Please refer to the notes below and

(c)   enter the employee's total gross earnings for the period *before* deducting P.A.Y.E., national insurance and any voluntary deductions. If none, enter "NIL"

(c)   total gross earnings   £ [ ][ ] p [ ][ ]

Notes:

(i)   **include** all payments (whenever paid), relating to this period including any overtime pay, shift premium, bonus, commission, etc.

(ii)   **exclude** payments paid in this period but relating to other periods, such as arrears, advances, or pay for holiday or sickness absence outside this period.

(iii)   **do not include** the value of benefits in kind, except as in (iv) below.

(iv)   *for agricultural, catering, etc., workers only,* include the reckonable value, laid down in the appropriate wages order, of accommodation, meals etc., provided by the employer.

(v)   **exclude** reimbursements or payments of travelling, subsistence, etc., expenses incurred in carrying out the employer's business.

2. Overtime earnings and overtime hours

(a)   Please enter the amount of overtime earnings for this period included in the total earnings at 1(c) above. If none, enter "NIL" (Enter all pay for overtime hours, not just the premium element).

(a)   overtime earnings   £ [ ][ ] p [ ][ ]

(b)   Please enter the number of actual hours of overtime work for which these overtime earnings were paid. If none, enter "NIL" (If, for example, 4 hours were paid at time and a half, **enter 4, not 6**).

(b)   overtime hours   Hours [ ][ ] Mins [ ][ ]

3. Payment by results, bonuses, shift premium payments, etc.

Please enter any payments of the following kinds included in the total earnings for this period at 1 (c) above, but not included in the overtime earnings at 2 (a) above.

(a)   Payments by results (e.g. piecework); bonuses (including profit-sharing); commission; and other incentive payments. If none, enter "NIL"

(a)   £ [ ][ ] p [ ][ ]

(b)   Premium payments (not total pay) for shift work, and for night work or weekend work where these are not treated as overtime. If none, enter "NIL"

(b)   £ [ ][ ] p [ ][ ]

NES 1978   **PLEASE TURN OVER**

✱Please answer the questions marked ✱ by putting a circle round the number to the right of the answer which applies.
(e.g. In answer to question 7 (a) put ① for a male but ② for a female).

4. Normal basic hours

Basic hours per week

	Hours	Mins

(a)   Please enter the number of hours which this employee is expected to work in a normal week
excluding main meal breaks
and *excluding* all overtime hours, even if these are worked regularly or contractually.

(a)

✱(b)   If, however, it is not possible to give a specific number of hours **because of the nature of the job** please indicate whether the employee is regarded as a full-time or part-time worker.

✱(b)   full-time 1
part-time 2

5. Wages Board or Council

If this employee is within the scope of a statutory Wages Board or Council
(even though other negotiated arrangements may more directly affect the pay and conditions of employment of the employee)
please enter its number from list 1 in the accompanying leaflet.   Otherwise, enter "NA"

6. Collective agreements.

✱(a)   Please indicate the type of negotiated collective agreement,
if any, which affects the pay and conditions of employment ✱(a)
of this employee, either directly or indirectly.
Please refer to the notes in the accompanying leaflet.

national agreement and supplementary
company / district / local agreement 1

national agreement only 2

company / district / local agreement only 3

no collective agreement 4

(b)   If one of the major agreements in list 2 in the accompanying leaflet affects the pay
and conditions of employment of this employee, either directly or indirectly,
please enter its number from the list.   Otherwise, enter "NA"   (b)

7. Sex and year of birth

✱(a)   Please indicate the sex of this employee.

✱(a)   male 1
female 2

(b)   Please enter the employee's year of birth. (If this question presents difficulty please give an estimate)   (b)   1 9

8. Location of workplace

Please refer to list 3 in the accompanying leaflet and enter the name of the London Borough or the names of the town or district
and also the county etc., in which the employee works or, if mobile, is based.

(a) In Greater London, the Borough of ....

(b) In England or Wales, ... Town/District in .... County

(c) In Scotland, ... Town/District in .... Region

9. Occupation

Please refer to the notes in the
accompanying leaflet and enter:—

(a)   the employee's job title,

(b)   a brief description of the work
and

(a)   Job title

(b)   Description

✱(c)   whether the employee has been doing work of the kind described
for at least 12 months in your employment.

✱(c)   At least 12 months 1
Under 12 months 2

Please nominate a person to deal with any queries about this completed form

.... C ....

.... J ....

.... E ....

Name ....Telephone ....

.... A ....

Date .... Signed on behalf of employer ....

.... O ....

APPENDIX E.   *The 1968 NES questionnaire*

Sheet No............   Line No..........

Department of Employment and Productivity

FOR OFFICIAL USE

To:— Name of employer	Batch and Sequence No......	1—6
.... Employer's business	Card Type .... Ø 1	7—8

PARTICULARS OF EMPLOYEE

Address at which employed	NI No.	9—17
.... Works number (if any)	Surname and initials	18—29
L O address stamp	LO Code No........	30—36
	MLH......	37—40
	WB	41—43 &

SPECIMEN

Dear Sir(s),

STATISTICS OF TRADE ACT, 1947

Notice under Section 1

This is to give you notice that the Secretary of State for Employment and Productivity requires you to furnish the information asked for in the following pages in respect of the employee named above. The form should be completed even if the employee has now left your employment. The information asked for is required for the appreciation of economic trends.

One copy of the form, when completed, should be returned to the Manager of the Employment Exchange at the address shown above. Exceptionally, it may be sent directly to the Department of Employment and Productivity Headquarters, Statistics Division, Orphanage Road, Watford, Herts., if special circumstances make this course more acceptable. The copy should be returned as soon as possible and in any case within 3 weeks of receiving this notice. The second copy is for your retention.

The information furnished will be regarded as strictly confidential and care will be taken that, in any statistics published, figures relating to an individual employee or to a firm or undertaking will not be disclosed.

Yours faithfully,

J. C. Barnes.

Permanent Under Secretary of State,
Department of Employment and Productivity.

E.S.2.

Please provide the following information about the **employee named on the front of this form** by entering the details requested, or by putting a tick in the box which applies.

The form should be completed whether or not this person is still in your employment. The information given should relate to the pay period which includes 25th September, 1968, or, if the employee was not then in your employment, to the pay period in your employment nearest to that date.

SECTION A—PARTICULARS OF EMPLOYEE AND CONDITIONS OF SERVICE

1 Place of work Please give the address of the employee's place of work or base if this is different from the employer's address shown on the front:—

....

.... **Ø2** 7—8

	Day	Month	Year

2 Age (a) Please state date of birth, if known...............................   9—14

or (b) show estimated age by ticking the appropriate box...............

	Under 18	18—20	21—24	25—29	30—39	40—49	50—59	60—64	65 and over
	1	2	3	4	5	6	7	8	9

15

	Male	Female
	1	2

3 Sex Please tick the appropriate box...   16

4 Occupation

(a) In your organisation what is this employee's job called? (If subject to a Wages Board or Council Order give job description under the Order)

(b) What are the employee's duties?

SPECIMEN

(c) Please indicate by ticking the appropriate box whether the employee is an apprentice, a trainee other than an apprentice, or neither

APPRENTICE	3
TRAINEE	2
NEITHER	1

17

(d) On pages 9 & 10 there is a list of the main occupations, in alphabetical order within 11 main groups. Each occupation is numbered. Please enter in the box below the number of the occupation which most nearly describes the job that this employee is doing. If an apprentice or trainee enter the number of the occupation for which he or she is training. A craftsman's mate should be coded 869 or 870 as appropriate.

OCCUPATION NUMBER [   ]   18—20

5 Current period in your employment

(a) Please enter the number of completed years in the current period in your employment If less than one enter "O"   [   ]   21—22

(b) Is the employee engaged by you for temporary employment, i.e. only for a limited period of under 6 months?

Yes	No
1	2

23

6 Particulars of working week (excluding overtime)

(a) Please tick the box which describes this employee's working arrangements

Day worker, basic hours usually spread over							Shift worker	Any other arrangement
Less than 4 days	4 days	4½ days	5 days	5½ days	6 days	as needed		
1	2	3	4	5	6	7	8	9

24

(b) How many hours is he or she normally expected to work, excluding overtime and main meal breaks?

Hours	Mins

25—28

3

7 Paid holidays Please state the number of days **paid** holidays to which this employee is currently entitled for :—

(a) Bank holidays (including any extra days) .... [   ] 29—30

(b) Annual holidays (measured in working days) .... [   ] 31—32

8 Other Benefits

(a) Please indicate, by ticking the appropriate box or boxes, whether any of the following benefits are provided by the employer to this employee, in addition to his gross pay. Benefits provided under the terms of a statutory wages order should be regarded as "free" for this purpose.

FREE FULL BOARD [   ] 33

FREE HOUSING OR ACCOMMODATION [   ] 34

FREE LUNCHEONS OR LUNCHEON VOUCHERS [   ] 35

(b) Does the employer provide this employee with any other income in kind which is estimated to be worth more than £1 a week to the employee?

Yes	No
1	2

36

If so, please give details below.

....
....
....
....

SECTION B—HOURS OF WORK AND PAY

If the employee is paid **weekly** the information given in this Section should relate to the pay week which Includes **25th September, 1968.** If paid **for any period other than a week**, it should relate to the pay period ended nearest to **30th September, 1968.** If the employee was not employed by you for the whole of this particular period information should be given in respect of the nearest complete pay period in your employment.

9 Please give the following particulars of the pay period for which you are providing information :—

(a) Period of :— 1 WEEK .... [ ] 1

FORTNIGHT .... [ ] 2

... WEEKS .... [ ] 3

5 WEEKS .... [ ] 4   37

CALENDAR MONTH .... [ ] 5

QUARTER .... [ ] 6

OTHER, PLEASE SPECIFY .... [ ] 7

Tick which box applies

....

(b) Period ended on ....

Day	Month	Year
		6 8

38—43

10 (a) Are the hours of work of this employee recorded for pay purposes?

Yes	No
1	2

44

(b) If so, how many hours did he or she work * in the period including any overtime?

Hours	Mins

45—49

(c) If, under "guaranteed week" or "guaranteed minimum overtime" arrangements, further hours were paid for though not worked, please enter the number of hours

Hours	Mins

50—53

The hours entered here should be actual hours, not pay hours, e.g. 4 hours worked and paid for at time and a half should be included as 4 and not 6.

4

11 Please show the make-up of the employee's total gross pay for the period shown in answer to
    Question 9.
    If hours of work are not recorded for pay purposes ignore columns (1) and (2) but complete
    column (3).
    If basic pay is calculated by multiplying an hourly rate by hours worked complete all 3 columns.
    In any other circumstances ignore column (1) but complete columns (2) and (3).

	1	2		3		
	Basic hourly rate (to nearest 'd')	Hours of work		Pay		
	s | d	Hours	Mins	£	s	d

(a) **Basic pay and hours** Hourly rate (i.e. on which overtime is or would be calculated); hours actually worked, excluding overtime; and pay for those hours. — 54—68

(b) **Overtime pay and hours** Actual hours of overtime* worked in excess of the basic hours shown in (a) above and pay for these overtime hours. — 69—79 **&** Ø3 7—8

(c) **Shift work pay etc** Premium payments for shift work, nightwork or weekend work within the normal working week. — 9—14

(d) **Payment by results** Amount paid under payment by results system linked to ......(i) individual effort .... — 15—20

(ii) group effort .... — 21—26

(iii) plant performance .... — 27—32

(iv) other systems .... — 33—38

(e) **Commission** .... — 39—45

(f) **Bonuses and/or profit sharing** (*Amounts included at (d) or (k) should not be entered here*) — 46—52

(g) **Pay under guarantee arrangements** Additional payments under "guaranteed week" or "guaranteed minimum overtime" arrangements. — 53—58

(h) (i) Holiday pay for holiday within the pay period .... — 59—65

(ii) Holiday pay for holiday outside the pay period .... — 66—72 **&** Ø4 7—8 9—15

(j) Arrears or advance of pay .... — 16—22

(k) Other payments (see Question 12) .... — 23—29

TOTAL GROSS PAY IN THE PERIOD (This total should agree with the employer's record)

The hours of overtime entered here should be actual hours, not pay hours, e.g. 4 hours worked and paid for at time and a half should be entered as 4 and not 6.

12 **Particulars of other payments.** Please indicate whether this employee's pay includes a specific payment for any item listed below. Tick in column A if payment for an item is included in the amount shown as basic pay in Question 11(a), or in column K if it is included in the amount shown as "Other payments" in Question 11(k).

	Col A		Col K	
MERIT ALLOWANCE	01		21	
SENIORITY OR AGE ALLOWANCE	02		22	
AREA ADDITION (E.G. LONDON WEIGHTING)	03		23	
COST OF LIVING ALLOWANCE	04		24	
LIEU ALLOWANCE	05		25	30—39
GOOD TIME-KEEPING ALLOWANCE	06		26	
DANGER MONEY, DIRTY MONEY..................................	07		27	
RESPONSIBILITY OR INCONVENIENCE PAY	08		28	
SITE ALLOWANCE OR FLAT-RATE TRAVELLING ALLOWANCE	09		29	
TOOL MONEY OR UNIFORM ALLOWANCE	10		30	
OTHER	11		31	

5

13 Loss of pay   If, in the pay period, this employee was paid for less than his or her normal basic hours, please indicate the reason by ticking the appropriate box or giving details.

SHORT-TIME WORKING, PLANT BREAKDOWN. INCLEMENT WEATHER	40
HOLIDAYS OR LEAVE, TIME OFF FOR STUDY OR OTHER APPROVED ABSENCE	41
CERTIFICATED SICKNESS, UNPAID OR ON REDUCED PAY	42
UNCERTIFICATED SICKNESS, UNPAID OR ON REDUCED PAY	43
VOLUNTARY ABSENTEEISM	44
LATE ARRIVAL, EARLY FINISH...	45
OTHER REASON (PLEASE GIVE DETAILS)	46

14 Shift pay over the shift cycle   Please state the average amount of shift premium per pay period paid to this employee over the full shift cycle.

£	s	d	
			47—52

15 Periodic payments of commission and bonuses   Please give particulars of payments of commission and/or bonus to this employee during the past year or a shorter **representative** period :—

	Total amount in year or shorter representative period			Period covered	
	£	s	d	Weeks	
COMMISSION					53—61 / Ø5 7—8
CHRISTMAS OR OTHER ANNUAL BONUS....					9—17
OTHER BONUS OR PROFIT SHARING					18—26

16 Other matters affecting pay

		Yes	No	
(a)	Does this employee normally receive tips or gratuities in addition to pay?	1	2	27
(b)	Were this employee's earnings during the relevant period adversely affected by lack of experience or practice because he or she had recently started on a new type of work?	1	2	28
(c)	To the employer's knowledge has this employee any mental or physical handicap which affects his or her capacity to earn?	1	2	29
(d)	Are there any other special circumstances which might affect this employee's level of pay and which are not already provided for elsewhere in the questionnaire?	1	2	30

If so, please give details below :-

....

....

....

....

SECTION C—PARTICULARS OF COLLECTIVE AGREEMENTS
OR STATUTORY WAGES REGULATION ORDERS AFFECTING PAY, ETC.

17 On pages 11 and 12 there is a list of the main national collective agreements, including those which apply to non-manual workers, and also the main statutory wage regulation orders which are laid down by Wages Boards and Councils.

(a) If the pay, normal hours of work or other conditions of employment of this employee are affected by* a national agreement and/or statutory order **in the list,** please write the number of that agreement or order or both in the box below.
If more than one **agreement** applies enter the number of the one most affecting **pay.**

AGREEMENT	31—33
ORDER	34—36

(b) If the employee's pay and conditions are affected by* a national agreement and/or statutory order which is **not in the list,** please give the title of the agreement or order or both and tick the appropriate box.

.... AGREEMENT   37

.... ORDER   38

(c) If the employee's pay and conditions are not affected by any national agreement or statutory order, please tick this box.

39

*In the sense that the centrally determined arrangements either provide the basis for actual pay and conditions of employment in the plant or establishment or, alternatively, provide a minimum standard, even though the employer may be operating a district, company, plant or establishment agreement which is more favourable to the employee.

18 If a national agreement and/or order has been quoted in answer to Question 17, and a standard or basic rate of pay or minimum entitlement for the employee's grade is laid down in the agreement or order or both, please quote the rate(s) either per year, per week or per hour†. Fractions of a penny should be rounded to the nearest penny. **Exclude** overtime payments. **Include** the value of any additional allowances paid to the employee under the terms of the agreement or order, such as cost of living supplements, premium or lead rates, basic piecework payments and premium pay for basic hours.

Laid down in national agreement

Rate........   £ s d   per..........

Year	1
Week	2
Hour	3

40—47

Number of hours per week (if rate quoted is per year or per week)..............

Hours	Mins

48—51

Laid down in statutory order

Rate................   £ s d   per..........

Week	1
Hour	2

52—57

Number of hours per week (if rate quoted is per week)........

Hours	Mins

58—61

†For an employee on a salary scale please quote the rate for the appropriate scale point, not the minimum of the scale

19 Are you, the employer, a member of an employers' organisation which is a party to the national **agreement,** if any, quoted in answer to question 17? Please tick the appropriate item.

Yes	No	Not applicable
3	2	1

62

7

20   If this employee is paid a basic rate different from the national rate quoted in answer to Question 18, or if no national rate has been quoted, please indicate, by ticking one or more of the boxes below, how his or her basic pay is determined :—

                   BY DISTRICT AGREEMENT   63

                   BY COMPANY AGREEMENT   64

                   BY LOCAL PLANT OR ESTABLISHMENT AGREEMENT   65

                   BY WORKPLACE AGREEMENT WITHIN THE PLANT OR ESTABLISHMENT   66

                   BY OTHER ARRANGEMENT   67

21   Where possible and relevant please indicate by ticking whether the basic rate of pay of this employee is regarded as a :—

                                         SKILLED RATE   1

                                         SEMI-SKILLED RATE   2   68 &

                                         UNSKILLED RATE   3

SECTION D

Please use this space for any comment or explanation you would like to make in connection with the answers given in this questionnaire.

SPECIMEN

Signed on behalf of employer ....   Date ....

      Name and telephone number of person to whom any queries about the questionnaire should be addressed.

Name ....   Tel No. ....

FOR OFFICIAL USE ONLY

LO comments.

Signature..   Date......................

APPENDIX F. *List of tables in British Labour Statistics Historical Abstract 1886—1968.*

Wage rates and normal hours

Table no.

1 Rates of wages and weekly hours of work in engineering in selected years, fitters and turners 1851–1968 and labourers 1920–1968

2 Rates of wages and weekly hours of work in the building industry in selected years, bricklayers 1810–1968

3 Rates of wages and weekly hours of work in the building industry in selected years, bricklayers' labourers 1810–1968

4 Rates of wages and weekly hours of work in the printing industry in selected years, compositors 1780–1968

5 Rates of wages and weekly hours of work in furniture manufacture in selected years, journeymen 1810–1968

6 Rates of wages and weekly hours of work in footwear manufacture in selected years, adult male workers 1810–1968

7 Wage rates in agriculture 1850–1914: average weekly cash wages of ordinary labourers

8 Wage rates and basic hours in agriculture 1914–1968: adult male workers

9 Rates of wages in certain occupations and industries 1914–1938: adult workers

10 Basic weekly rates of wages for men laid down in selected collective agreements or statutory orders 1947–1968

11 Index of weekly wage rates 1874–1914

Table no.

12 Percentage change in weekly wage rates 1914–1920

13 Indices of basic weekly rates of wages, all manual workers, all industries and services 1920–1968

14 Indices of basic weekly rates of wages, manual workers; men, women, juveniles and all workers, all industries and services 1947–1955

15 Indices of basic weekly rates of wages, manual workers; men, women, juveniles and all workers, all industries and services 1956–1968

16 Indices of basic weekly rates of wages, manual workers; men, women, juveniles and all workers, manufacturing industries 1947–1955

17 Indices of basic weekly rates of wages, manual workers; men, women, juveniles and all workers, manufacturing industries 1956–1968

18 Indices of basic weekly rates of wages, all manual workers, by industry 1947–1955

19 Indices of basic weekly rates of wages, all manual workers, by industry 1956–1968

20 Indices of normal weekly hours of work, all manual workers, all industries and services 1920–1968

21 Indices of normal weekly hours of work, manual workers; men, women, juveniles and all workers, all industries and services 1947–1955

Vacancies and placings

Household and family expenditure surveys

Table no.

Size of manufacturing establishments

SUBJECT INDEX TO WAGES AND EARNINGS

157